AAT

AF622503

Level 4

Professional Accounting Technician Apprenticeship

Systems and Processes

Course Book

For Assessments from September 2026

BPP
LYCEUM EDUCATION GROUP

First edition 2026

ISBN 9781 0355 4448 6

ISBN (for internal use only) 9781 0355 4068 6

eISBN 9781 0355 4469 1

British Library Cataloguing-in-Publication Data

A catalogue record for this book is available from the British Library

Published by

BPP Learning Media Ltd
BPP House, Aldine Place
142–144 Uxbridge Road
London W12 8AA

learningmedia.bpp.com

Your learning materials are printed on paper obtained from traceable sustainable sources.

We are grateful to the Association of Accounting Technicians for permission to reproduce past examination questions.

Contents

Introduction to the course

Syllabus overview

The purpose of the unit is to enable students to demonstrate their understanding of the role of the accounting function in an organisation and the importance of internal controls in minimising the risk of loss. Students will undertake an evaluation of an accounting system to identify weaknesses and assess the impact of those weaknesses on the operation of the organisation.

When organisations have a planned change in policy, there will be a transition period – which will present its own challenges. Students need to be able to review a planned change in policy, identify potential problem areas while one system is being changed to another and make suitable recommendations to ensure that the integrity of the accounting system is maintained.

The accounting system affects all areas of an organisation and should be capable of producing information to assist management with decision making, monitoring and control, as well as producing financial information to meet statutory obligations. In this unit, students will demonstrate analytical and problem-solving skills, exercising judgement to make informed recommendations. These are practical skills that are essential to the accounting technician.

Systems and Processes requires students to have a sound understanding of management accounting and financial accounting information requirements, and the way that the accounting function needs to support both areas.

This **Systems and Processes** unit is only examined as part of the **Professional Accounting Technician Apprenticeship Role Scenario**, along with knowledge and understanding of management accounting and financial statements from your previous studies.

Test specification for Professional Accounting Technician Apprenticeship Role Scenario

Role Scenario Assessment

The knowledge assessment will be administered in a controlled and invigilated environment. The role scenario is a key component of the EPA. The assessment will demonstrate that the apprentice can apply their knowledge in an integrated way and will satisfy the requirements specified in the standard.

Assessment method	Marking type	Duration of assessment	Total number of marks available
Computer-based role scenario assessment	Partially computer and partially human marked Results available four weeks from the date of assessment, following quality assurance processes by AAT	2 hours 30 minutes	60

Role scenario assessment specification

Assessment objective (AO)	Weighting	Total number of marks
AO1: Understand ethics and accounting fundamentals **K1** The principles of professional ethics and codes of conduct in an accounting environment, including approaches to interpreting ethics in complex situations **K2** Professional standards and legal regulations relevant to an organisation's financial information, such as accounting standards, ethical codes and internal principles **K4** Principles of double entry bookkeeping and accounting standards to create and report financial information to the users of accounts **K5** Principles of financial accounting for a range of single entities, eg sole traders, limited companies or partnerships, adjustment and reporting including standard year end journal entries and the correction of errors **S2** Apply accounting principles and adhere to legislation to ensure records are accurate and compliant with law or company policy when delivering accounting activities, such as the financial accounting of single entities, limited companies or partnerships or management accounting activities for an organisation	25%	15
AO2: Understand financial reporting **K7** Principles of interpretation of financial information for management accounts preparation or the drafting of financial statements, such as ratio analysis **S4** Interpret financial information for accounting purposes, such as using judgement to determine the correct way to report or account for transaction or undertaking ratio analysis	25%	15

Assessment objective (AO)	Weighting	Total number of marks
AO3: Understand the management accounting process **K6** Principles of management accounting eg, the purpose of management accounting, budgetary planning and control, costing, decision making **S1** Collate and analyse financial information and show how that information can be used most effectively to support value creation within an organisation **S7** Deliver accounting tasks with a critical eye to transactions and trends, demonstrating a 'right first time approach'	25%	15
AO4: Understand internal control systems **K8** Systems of risk management and financial control, and identification of potential vulnerabilities that could lead to issues such as internal fraud or money laundering **S3** Apply professional scepticism when undertaking accounting activities to inform and evaluate decision making on the content of true and fair accounts, being alert to conditions that may indicate possible misstatement of financial information due to error or fraud, establishing the facts sensitively and being aware of unconscious bias	25%	15

Failed assessments should be re-sat within the following timescales:

- For the role scenario assessment, a re-sit should be taken at the next available assessment opportunity and not more than six months after the EPA outcome notification. The timescale for a retake is dependent on how much training is required.
- For the professional discussion, a re-sit is typically taken within one month of the EPA outcome notification. The timescale for a re-take is dependent on how much re-training is required and is typically taken within three months of the EPA outcome notification.

Failed assessment methods must be re-sat or re-taken within six-month period from the EPA outcome notification, otherwise the entire EPA will need to be re-sat or re-taken in full.

Re-sits and re-takes are not offered to an apprentice wishing to move from pass to a higher grade.

Skills bank

Our experience of preparing students for this type of assessment suggests that to obtain competency, you will need to develop a number of key skills.

What do I need to know to do well in the AAT Professional Accounting Technician Apprenticeship Role Scenario

Systems and Processes is assessed in the Professional Accounting Technician Apprenticeship Role Scenario, along with other material from management accounting and financial accounting.

Assumed knowledge

The synoptic assessment will test the Systems and Processes material within this unit, along with some Management Accounting and Financial Accounting topics outlined in the assessment objectives.

Styles of questions

The following sections include guidance on the various types of task that you will find within the assessment.

Drop-down boxes

This type of task provides a number of options within a list. You need to click on the relevant box and then select the correct answer. Drop-down boxes could be used in stand-alone tasks – eg:

Louise Harding, the finance director of QSL Products Ltd (QSL), has asked you to analyse the published results of a competitor business.

Until recently, you were employed by that business. Therefore, you have a detailed understanding of its financial position.

(a) (i) **Which principle is threatened by this request?** **(1 mark)**

[▼]

(ii) **How should you respond?** **(1 marks)**

[▼]

Drop-down boxes could also be used within a table – eg:

Liz Hall, the accounts payable clerk, asks you for advice. She wants to know whether the following errors would be detected by completing a payable ledger control account reconciliation.

(c) **Identify whether the errors would be detected.** **(3 marks)**

Error	Would be detected/ would NOT be detected
A supplier invoice has been posted to the wrong supplier account.	▼
A cheque payment has been debited to the receivables ledger control account.	▼
A purchase invoice has been debited to the account of a supplier.	▼

Check-boxes

Tasks may require you to select the correct option by checking a box in the correct column within a table – eg:

(b) Identify whether the stakeholder is an internal or external stakeholder. (2 marks)

Stakeholder	Internal stakeholder	External stakeholder
Customer	O	O
Director	O	O

Gapfill or cell within a table

For some tasks, there will be cells within a table that you are expected to complete with the correct amount – usually based on some supporting calculations that you are expected to complete. These are most likely to appear in Tasks 2 and 3 when considering financial and management accounting tasks respectively.

Here is an example from the AAT Practice Assessment:

(a) Calculate the missing ratios. (Enter your answers to one decimal place.) (10 marks)

QSL Products Ltd scorecard

	Year ended 31 Dec 20X2	Year ended 31 Dec 20X1
Profitability and gearing		
Gross profit margin		28.4
Operating profit margin	2.2	6.3
Return on capital employed		17.5
Gearing	20.1	16.6
Liquidity		
Current ratio	:1	1.8:1
Acid test/quick ratio	:1	0.8:1
Working capital		
Inventory holding period (days)	94.2	92.1
Trade receivables collection period (days)	53.0	54.3
Trade payables payment period (days)	89.9	85.6
Working capital cycle (days)		60.8

Multiple-choice questions (MCQs)

Some tasks might require the selection of the correct option from a list including a number of incorrect options – eg:

(b) Identify the correct summary of QSL's performance against each of the following categories.

(i) Profitability **(1 mark)**

- ○ This has been a year of steady, if unspectacular, progress. Although profitability has dipped, the return on capital employed has been kept under control.
- ○ The profitability ratios give cause for concern. The small increase in sales revenue has not improved the gross profit percentage. Operating expenses have increased, reducing operating profit and return on capital employed.
- ○ Some profitability ratios have improved and some have deteriorated. Further investigation is required to understand whether profitability is improving.

Drag-and-drop

It is possible that there may be a task which requires you to drag the correct option from a list and place it beside the relevant section – eg:

(b) Match the stage of the product life cycle to each description. **(4 marks)**

Description	Stage
There is a steep upward trend in revenue.	
New products enter the market and demand starts to fall.	
Economies of scale are achieved, and advertising costs are low.	
There are high advertising costs but low revenue levels.	

Decline	Growth	Introduction	Maturity

Written tasks

You can expect to see at least one task where you are required to write your answer in a text box that is provided within the software – eg:

(d) (i) Identify THREE systemic weaknesses in the company's internal controls for handling purchases on credit. **(3 marks)**

(ii) Explain how each weakness that you have identified could create problems for the company. **(6 marks)**

Weakness 1
Potential problems for the company

Weakness 2
Potential problems for the company

Weakness 3
Potential problems for the company

In this case, you are being asked for three weaknesses and how they may cause problems for the company. Here, there is 1 mark available for the identification of the weakness and a further 2 marks to explain why this may be an issue for the company. Therefore, sufficient information must be written to explain the issue and why this may be the case, but there is no need to write an overly long explanation as the maximum points available are three marks per valid weakness.

Alternatively, the answer may require more detail, and a larger amount of space will be available to input your answer. Look carefully at the marking allocation to give an indication of the level of detail required.

How to approach written tasks

The main verbs used for these types of question requirement are:

- **Identify** – analyse and select for presentation
- **Explain** – set out in detail the meaning of
- **Discuss** – by argument, discuss the pros and cons

Here is a step-by-step approach that you can practise when attempting written tasks.

Step 1 **Read** the question carefully.

It is important to read the question carefully to identify exactly what is being asked of you. It is a good idea to highlight key words and all verbs as this will ensure you answer the question that is being asked, not the question you think they should ask!

Step 2 **Plan** your answer.

Once you have established the requirement, note down what you know about the topic, relevant to what is being asked (key words only). It is a good idea to do this on a piece of paper so you can eliminate irrelevant knowledge and formulate a logical answer when you enter it on screen.

Note down any key requirements (eg the answer format) and make sure you plan to say something about everything that the task requires.

Step 3 **Structure** your answer.

Before answering the question set, you need to carefully review the scenario given in order to consider what questions need to be answered, and what needs to be included in your answer. A simple framework that could be used to answer the question is as follows:

- Point – make the point
- Evidence – use information from the scenario as evidence
- Explain – explain why the evidence links to the point
- Recommend – if required, explain how the company in the scenario should proceed

Let's consider an **illustration** of this approach – if the task is to explain the net profit margin from the scenario:

- **Point**: The net profit margin (NPM) tell us the amount of net profit earned per pound of revenue.
- **Evidence**: In this case, the company is performing better than the competitor as we have a higher NPM percentage than theirs.
- **Explain**: '[...] which means that/the consequences are [...]'
- **Recommendation**: 'Therefore, we should invest in the company.'

This approach provides a formula or framework that can be followed, to answer written questions:

> The NPM tells us that [point ...] in this case the company is [evidence ...] which means that [explain ...] so we should/should not [recommendation ...].

You must familiarise yourself with the style of the online questions and the AAT software before taking the assessment. As part of your revision, login to the AAT website and attempt their online practice assessments.

Introduction to the assessment

Information on the scenario for your AAT Professional Accounting Technician Apprenticeship Synoptic Assessment is issued in advance of the assessment as preseen material. You must make sure you are familiar with the relevant pre-seen material before sitting your assessment. The pre-seen scenario for the live assessment should be downloaded from the AAT website here:

https://www.aat.org.uk/learningportal

Note that the scenario is also included as a pop-up in the live assessment, but it is strongly advised that you familiarise yourself with the information prior to the assessment.

It is also useful to familiarise yourself with the other introductory information you **may** be given at the start of the assessment. The following is provided at the beginning of the Professional Diploma Synoptic practice assessment:

You have **2 hours 30 minutes** to complete this **Role Scenario Practice Assessment**.

- This assessment contains **four tasks** and you should attempt to complete **every** task.
- Each task is independent. You will not need to refer to your answers to previous tasks.
- The total number of marks for this assessment is **60**.
- Read every task carefully to make sure you understand what is required.
- Where the date is relevant, it is given in the task data.
- Both minus signs and brackets can be used to indicate negative numbers **unless** task instructions state otherwise.
- You must use a comma to indicate a decimal point. For example, write 100.57 **not** 100,57 or 10057.
- You may use a comma to indicate a number in the thousands, but you don't have to. For example, 10000 and 10,000 are both acceptable.
- You will need to double click to enter values into a gapfill or cell within a table.

Once you have clicked 'Continue,' you will not be able to return to this page. You will be able to view the 'Assessment information' in the references section at each task position.

(a) Attempt as many tasks as possible in the **Exam Practice Kit**. There are plenty of assessment-style tasks which are excellent preparation for the real synoptic assessment.

(b) Always **check** through your own answers as you will in the real assessment, before looking at the solutions in the back of the **Exam Practice Kit.**

Key to icons

Key term

A key definition which is important to be aware of for the assessment.

Formula to learn

A formula you will need to learn as it will not be provided in the assessment.

Formula provided

A formula which is provided within the assessment and generally available as a pop-up on screen.

Activity

An example which allows you to apply your knowledge to the technique covered in the Course Book. The solution is provided at the end of the chapter.

Illustration

A worked example which can be used to review and see how an assessment question could be answered.

Assessment focus point

A high priority point for the assessment.

Open book reference

Where use of an open book will be allowed for the assessment.

Real life examples

A practical real life scenario.

AAT

Supplements

From time to time, we may need to publish supplementary materials to one of our titles. This can be for a variety of reasons – from a small change in the AAT unit guidance to new legislation coming into effect between editions.

You should check our supplements page regularly for anything that may affect your learning materials. All supplements are available free of charge on our supplements page on our website at: https://www.learningmedia.bpp.com/pages/resources-for-students

Improving material and removing errors

BPP Learning Media do everything possible to ensure the material is accurate and up to date when sending to print. In the event that any errors are found after the print date, they are uploaded to the following website: https://learningmedia.bpp.com/pages/errata.

These learning materials are based on the qualification specification released by the AAT in October 2025.

1 Reporting and stakeholders

Learning outcomes

1.1	**Understand the purpose of key financial reports and their use by a range of stakeholders** Students need to know: • The purpose and content of statutory financial statements • The purpose and content of financial information produced for internal use • The key external stakeholders of an organisation • How financial information is used by both internal and external stakeholders • The importance of ethical information and sustainability practices to internal and external stakeholders • The following types of financial report: - Statement of profit or loss - Statement of financial position - Statement of cash flow - Budgetary control reports

Assessment context

The topics covered in this chapter are most likely to be included in Task 1 of the Role Scenario Assessment, which tests understanding ethics and accounting fundamentals.

Qualification context

This chapter builds on content that you will have seen in your previous studies and will complement what you have learned at Level 4 in both Management Accounting and Financial Statements.

Business context

Accountants need to understand the purpose of the internal and external reports they create, and how this information will be used by a variety of stakeholders. When preparing reports, you must consider why the information is required, so that it can be provided in the appropriate format and with the appropriate level of detail, bearing in mind the needs of the reader(s) of the report. Given the increasing importance of both ethical and sustainability matters, it is no surprise that the modern-day accountant needs to be able to provide information that goes beyond the traditional core financial statements.

Chapter overview

Reporting and stakeholders

- **Stakeholders of organisations**
  - Types of stakeholder
  - Expectations of stakeholders
  - Information requirements of stakeholders
  - Internal stakeholders
  - External stakeholders
- **External reporting requirements**
  - Statutory financial statements
  - Tax regulations
  - Other government legislation
- **Internal reporting requirements**
  - Management accounting
  - Budgetary control reports
  - Scorecards
  - Management Information Systems (MIS)
    - Purposes of management information
    - Types of information
    - Information requirements in different sectors
- **Ethical and sustainability reporting**
  - Mission statement
  - Corporate social responsiblity (CSR) reporting
  - Sustainability reporting
  - Ethical reporting
  - Integrated reporting

Introduction

Within this chapter, you will learn about the various stakeholders that an organisation might have, and consider their expectations and their information needs. You will consider the differences between internal and external stakeholders as well as the differences between the internal and external reporting responsibilities facing organisations.

As part of these reporting responsibilities, you will revisit the various statutory financial statements and other necessary forms of communication before considering internal reporting tools such as management accounts, budgets, and scorecards.

Finally, you will consider reporting in ethical and sustainability terms, with reference to current trends and responsibilities.

1 Stakeholders of organisations

To understand why financial reports are produced, it is important to first consider who the users of these reports will be. Some reports are used for external reporting purposes (eg a statement of profit or loss) and others for internal use only (eg a budgetary control report).

1.1 Types of stakeholder

Stakeholder: Individuals or groups that, potentially, have an interest in what an organisation does.

A stakeholder is anyone who is affected by the actions of the organisation. A stakeholder can also affect the actions of the organisation due to their interest.

Stakeholders can be:

- Internal or external to the organisation – eg lenders (external) and shareholders (internal)
- Directly or indirectly affected by its actions – eg customers, suppliers, employees, beneficiaries
- Actively or passively able to affect the organisation – eg government, the natural environment

1.2 Expectations of stakeholders

Each type of stakeholder has a different role in relation to the organisation, and therefore has different expectations of the organisation. Let's consider this in the context of a typical business.

Stakeholders in the business	What is at stake?	What do they typically expect of the business?
Owners (shareholders), partners or proprietors	Money invested	A return on their investment so that their wealth increases: • Steady, growing profits paid out by the business • Growth in capital value of their share of the business
Directors/managers	Livelihoods, careers and reputations	Fair and growing remuneration
Employees and trade unions		Career progression Safe working environment Training Pension
Customers	Their custom The money they spend on products and services	Products/services that are of good quality and value Fair terms of trade plus continuity of supply
Suppliers and other business partners	The items they supply	Fair terms of trade plus continuity of custom Prompt payment
Lenders	Money lent and interest received	A return on their investment: • Interest • Repayment of capital

Stakeholders in the business	What is at stake?	What do they typically expect of the business?
Government and its agencies	National infrastructure used by business The welfare of employees Tax revenue	Reasonable employment and other business practices Steady or rising stream of tax revenue
The local community and the public at large	National infrastructure used by business The welfare of employees	Reasonable employment and other business practices Being a responsible organisation
The natural environment	The environment shared by all	Reasonable environmental and other practices

The key stakeholders can be mapped on **Mendelow's Matrix** in terms of:

- How **interested** they are in the organisation's activities (would they **want** to resist?)
- How much **power** they have over the organisation's activities (would they be **able** to resist?)

Power \ Level of interest	Low	High
Low	**Minimal Effort** Casual labour	**Keep Informed** Small local suppliers Core employees
High	**Keep Satisfied** Government Customers	**Key Players** Key managers/employees Main suppliers

Figure 1.1: Mendelow's Matrix

A stakeholder that has a **high level of interest** in the organisation and also a **high level of power** – for instance, a bank that has given the organisation a large overdraft and is concerned that it is about to be breached – should be regarded as a key player when it comes to giving it the information it seeks. Organisations in this position should make sure that they keep the bank well informed, and perhaps even involved in its decisions – eg authorising large items of capital expenditure.

Other stakeholders, with **lower levels of interest and/or power**, should simply be kept informed to the degree required by legislation or contractual requirements eg small shareholders should be sent copies of the annual financial statements and invited to the annual general meeting as required by company law.

1.3 Information requirements of stakeholders

Each type of stakeholder has a **different role** in relation to the organisation and, therefore, has **different informational needs**.

Organisations need to **communicate appropriately** with stakeholders.

1.4 Internal stakeholders

KEY TERM

> **Internal stakeholders:** A category of stakeholders that includes employees, management, and owners (eg shareholders).

They will require different types of information, depending on their role within the organisation, for example **management and owners** will want to know how the organisation is performing but will not necessarily need to have a detailed view of what payments any given customer has made on their account. Equally, a **payables ledger clerk** will need to know which invoices are required to be paid on the next payment run, and so will need a detailed schedule for review on a supplier - by-supplier basis.

Information provided to internal stakeholders is **not formalised by regulatory or legal guidance**; instead, the users will dictate what information they require and how they want this to be presented to ensure the most efficient way of using it for their own needs.

Internal stakeholders may be using the system to ensure that they can perform their jobs correctly. For example, **warehouse staff** will need to be able to access the inventory system to check availability or location of products, and **sales staff** will need to be able to access price and available stock information, as well as accounts receivable information to ensure that any credit extended to customers is appropriate.

Staff hours are increasingly being logged using automated systems, such as a **swipe-cards** in factories and **online timesheets** for office-based staff. This is useful information for management as they pay staff for the hours they have worked, but they can also ensure accurate costing of finished goods (labour rates and efficiencies) and job costings (such as solicitors' and accountants' charge out rates).

Activity 1: Internal stakeholders

Consider the following list of internal stakeholders. Note down the information which they would specifically require as employees of CCC.

(1) Directors of CCC

(2) Joe Bloggins in his role as warehouse manager

(3) Joe Bloggins in his role as operations manager

(4) Wages clerk

Required

Explain how each of the stakeholders above would use the information they require and, where appropriate, consider any risks to the business if the information they receive is inaccurate or late.

1.5 External stakeholders

KEY TERM

> **External stakeholders:** A group of stakeholders that includes customers, suppliers, banks and public groups, including government.

They will usually require a **more formal** and **standardised reporting format**. If the organisation has a bank loan or overdraft, the bank will want to review the financial statements as well as any business forecasts.

Statutory financial reports must be filed with the Registrar of Companies on an annual basis in line with the Companies Act 2006 and appropriate accounting standards and policies.

The **natural environment** is also an external stakeholder but does not usually have any information needs of its own – however, those that act on its behalf (eg regulators, campaigners and environmental pressure groups) may still require information of some kind (eg data on sewage discharges) due to their interest in the organisation and its actions.

Activity 2: External stakeholders

Using the pre-seen information provided on CCC, identify the key external stakeholders who would require information regularly from the company. Briefly explain why these stakeholders would require this information.

2 External reporting requirements

Financial reports are used by internal and external stakeholders. **External reports** will generally have to adhere to a set of reporting requirements laid down in company law and presented in accordance with the applicable financial reporting framework. **Internal reports** can be less formalised and will be set out according to the type and the needs of the individual organisation.

You will have covered the content, legal and regulatory requirements of external reports in Level 4 Financial Statements.

2.1 Statutory financial statements

International Financial Reporting Standards (IFRS® Accounting Standards) are updated regularly. As such, it is important that any organisation which uses them to compile their financial statements can accurately compile the financial information.

The purpose and importance of statutory financial statements prepared in accordance with the Companies Act 2006 and accounting standards has been covered in Level 4 Financial Statements. Here is a brief recap of the key purposes:

(a) To determine whether the organisation has made a profit or a loss

(b) To demonstrate how well (or otherwise) the directors have exercised their management or stewardship of the company's resources

(c) To meet the company's statutory requirement to prepare financial statements that show a true and fair view of its financial performance during a period, and its financial position at the end of it

(d) To help shareholders (and potential new investors) evaluate how far their capital invested in the company is at risk, and determine the return they should be expecting to compensate them for this risk

(e) To help lenders and suppliers determine whether the company will be able to meet its financial commitments as they fall due

The statutory financial statements comprise the following:

KEY TERM

Statement of financial position: A list of all of the assets, liabilities and equity of the business at a particular point in time (the end of the reporting period).

Statement of profit or loss: A summary of the activity of the company during the reporting period (usually a year) comprising income and expenditure.

Statement of changes in equity: A reconciliation of the opening and closing equity balances for the reporting period. It enables stakeholders to see the impact of new share issues, profit or loss for the period and dividends paid to equity shareholders.

Statement of cash flows: An analysis of how and why the company's cash balance has changed during a reporting period. In addition to the statement of financial position and the statement of profit or loss, it is important for both management and current and potential investors to understand how cash is being utilised by the business.

Activity 3: Financial statements

CCC has a December year end. The pre-seen information has extracts from the previous year's financial statements.

Required

Explain which financial statements which would be most useful to the external stakeholders identified earlier in this chapter.

As part of your explanation, you should highlight any potential issues that may arise in respect of these stakeholders using the financial statements and whether any further information will be required by them in addition to the financial statements.

Activity 4: Cash flows

The following is an extract from the statement of cash flows produced by CCC as at 31 December 20X2. It was produced as part of the pack supplied by the external accountants, Bright & Co. The Cookridge brothers are very pleased to have a statement of cash flows – however, they are unsure how to interpret it.

CCC Ltd

Statement of cash flows for the year ended 31 December 20X2

	£	£
Cash flows from operating activities		
Profit before tax		2,000
Add back:		
– Depreciation for 20X2	7,000	
– Finance costs	5,000	
– Increase in inventory	(24,000)	
– Increase in trade receivables	(51,000)	
– Increase in accruals	2,000	
– Increase in trade payables	45,000	
		(16,000)
Cash used in operating activities		(14,000)
Less: Interest paid	(5,000)	
Net cash used in operating activities		(19,000)
Cash flows from investing activities		
Purchase of non-current assets	(2,000)	
Net cash used in investing activities		(2,000)

	£	£
Cash flows from financing activities		
Receipt of loan	60,000	
Net cash generated from financing activities		60,000
Net increase in cash and cash equivalents		39,000
Cash and cash equivalents @ 1 January 20X2		(74,000)
Cash and cash equivalents @ 31 December 20X2		(35,000)

Required

Briefly explain the significance of the key figures in the CCC statement of cash flows as at 31 December 20X2. (Use specific examples from the statement to support your answer.)

2.2 Tax regulations

Financial statements are not the only external reporting requirement; the local tax authorities will need to ensure that the organisation is paying sufficient tax based on their profits for the period.

The main taxes for organisations are **employment taxes** (PAYE and NICs) **corporation tax** and value added tax (VAT). You will not be asked detailed computational questions in your assessment, but you will need to understand the reporting implications on the organisation.

HMRC require most employers to report their payroll deductions on a monthly basis, using real-time information (RTI). This requires organisations to use software that can report this information to HMRC online. It also requires organisations to report on a timely basis, placing both technological and staff burdens on businesses, as information is required prior to payments to staff being made.

VAT must also be reported electronically for all VAT-registered businesses, again requiring upgraded software (or even new software in some cases) and additional training time for staff.

2.3 Other government legislation

Pensions legislation has been introduced whereby employers are required to auto-enrol their staff into stakeholder pension schemes. This has resulted in additional financial burdens (payment of contributions) and administrative burdens (ensuring all staff are enrolled within the reporting deadlines and submitting the required returns to the Pensions Regulator) on the payroll staff within the finance function.

Money Laundering Regulations were updated in 2017, requiring organisations to register with a supervisory authority (eg the AAT) and ensuring compliance with the strict reporting criteria, as well as organisations to ensure additional training of staff to identify and prevent the main elements of money laundering or terrorist financing. In particular, the Regulations require an organisation to have documented policies, controls and procedures in place to prevent activities related to money laundering (Law Society, 2020).

3 Internal reporting requirements

3.1 Management accounting

Management accounts are not bound by regulation and are intended to meet the needs primarily of the company's management.

The types of management accounting report are covered in depth in Level 4 Management Accounting.

These include the preparation of information such as:

- Budgets
- Standard costs
- Variance analysis
- Ratio analysis
- Sales figures for products and/or divisions
- Inventory levels
- Profitability reports
- Any other internal information prepared using financial data

Management accounting reports will be used internally by decision makers to help them:

(a) **Make decisions** on resourcing and resource allocation

(b) **Manage the company's profitability and cash flow**

For example, strong accounts receivable and credit control systems will ensure that prompt payment ('settlement') discounts are taken up when available, and creditors are paid on time.

(c) **Monitor** the controls and review any areas for unusual or unexpected results which may highlight business-critical issues, control issues or potential fraud

This is covered in more detail in Chapter 2.

Organisations should be taking advantage of available tax incentives, too. For example, when considering a new large non-current asset to be purchased, what are the capital allowances available? Does this affect the decision to proceed with the purchase?

Management must carefully monitor the spending of government grants to ensure adequate reporting in the financial statements as well as accurate comparison of actuals against budget.

3.2 Budgetary control reports

A key report issued by the management accounting function is the **budgetary control report**, or **variance analysis** report.

A budgetary control report compares standard costs and revenues with actual results to obtain variances which highlight any deviations that managers should investigate to improve performance.

Activity 5: CCC budgetary control report

Below is the budgetary control report for the newly launched Wood Effect (Oak) in the Umteeko range for Quarter 1 of 20X3. CCC only prepares this once a quarter due to the level of work required and the ability of the staff to complete this in addition to their current workloads.

Stefan, who has some AAT training, is responsible for completing this analysis. Stefan does not fully understand how fixed costs are absorbed, so he has left those bits blank for now. Stefan has included the cost of delivery and motor expenses in the variable cost calculation.

This analysis covers only the best-selling products and is passed to the directors for their review. However, Stefan is unsure as to which areas are of most interest to the directors.

CCC Ltd

Budgetary control report for Umteeko Oak the three months to March 20X3

	£	£	£	
Budgeted profit			21,000	
Sales volume profit variance			1,750	(Favourable)
Standard profit from actual sales			22,750	
	Favourable	**Adverse**		
Variances				
Sales price	975			
Material price	200			
Material usage		7,500		
Labour rate	600			
Labour efficiency		4,250		
Variable overhead rate	125			
Variable overhead efficiency	350			
Fixed overhead expenditure	–			
Fixed overhead volume efficiency	–			
Fixed overhead volume capacity	–			
	2,250	11,750	9,500	(Adverse)
Actual profit			13,250	

Required

(a) Identify areas on which the directors should focus in more detail in the above budgetary control report.

(b) Comment on any limitations on the above budgetary information supplied.

The mechanics of how the standard costs are determined, and how the associated variances are calculated, are covered in Level 4 Management Accounting, so are not covered here. The management accounting unit also covers the meaning of these variances, and how they complement each other.

Understanding and communicating these aspects of the budgetary control report are vital roles of the accounting function.

3.3 Scorecards

KEY TERM

> **Scorecard:** A performance management tool which addresses all relevant areas of performance, both financial and non-financial, in an objective and unbiased fashion.

It is increasingly common for management accounting functions to produce scorecards incorporating **both financial and non-financial ratios, and other indicators**.

A scorecard should provide managers with information which addresses all relevant areas of performance, and in an objective and unbiased fashion.

Scorecards differ from financial reporting in that they include non-financial information too.

Scorecards typically contain measures from at least four different **perspectives**, commonly including:

(a) **Customer satisfaction** – on issues that matter to customers (cost, quality, delivery, inspection, query handling, etc)

(b) **Process efficiency** – with the aim of improving internal processes, decision making and resource utilisation

(c) **Growth** – or the business's capacity to maintain its competitive position through the acquisition of new skills (training) and the development of new products (innovation

(d) **Financial success** – including traditional measures, such as growth, profitability and shareholder value, with a clear focus on how value is created for all major stakeholders

The scorecard can be used to identify suitable **targets** for each measure, commensurate with the company's overall strategy. These targets can be cascaded to departmental managers, who are responsible for achieving them. In doing so goal congruence is embedded within the control system.

The **advantages** of the scorecard approach:

- It looks at both internal and external matters concerning the company.
- It is related to the key elements of a company's strategy.
- Financial and non-financial measures are linked together.
- There is a recognition that financial success is driven by non-financial factors, such as innovation, customer satisfaction and internal efficiency.

Activity 6: Balanced scorecard and ratios

Below is a balanced scorecard drawn up by John Cookridge for CCC.

He has drawn up some of the objectives and how these can be measured.

Financial success		Customer satisfaction	
Objectives	**Measures**	**Objectives**	**Measures**
To be profitable	Financial results	Great service Excellent range of quality products	Repeat business New products that sell to the local customer base

Process efficiency		Growth	
Objectives	**Measures**	**Objectives**	**Measures**
Efficient staff	Staff meeting realistic targets for fitting and delivery times	Trained staff	Employees with relevant training and qualifications
Ethical treatment of suppliers	Pay suppliers on time	Becoming the largest independent flooring provider in the region	Increase in market share

Required

Using the information regarding the objectives and measures used by CCC in its balanced scorecard, together with financial information in the scenario, answer the following:

(a) **Comment on the profitability of the company, using appropriate ratios with explanations.**

(b) **Consider the customer satisfaction objectives and measures used by CCC and make recommendations on how the company can improve data and feedback on them to management.**

(c) **CCC bases its process efficiency measures on the efficiency of staff and paying suppliers on time. Using ratios where appropriate, analyse whether CCC are meeting these objectives.**

(d) **Using the stated objectives used by CCC regarding its growth metrics, make recommendations on how the company can improve on its reporting measures, ensuring management obtain accurate and useful information.**

3.4 Management information systems (MIS)

Management information is information provided to management to help them with planning, controlling, performance measurement and decision making.

Most of the information produced by the accounting function for both internal and external stakeholders is based on data about the transactions that it has processed over a given period. These are recorded in the accounting system, which we will look at in Chapter 3.

However, some of the data comes from the wider management information system (MIS) which is the processing of the various information using computers (or computer software) from multiple departments or functions. This is particularly the case when the accounting function is preparing information for its key internal stakeholder, the management of the company.

3.4.1 Purposes of management information

All companies require management information for a range of purposes including:

Planning	To plan effectively, managers need information that helps them make decisions about what should and can be done bearing in mind: • The resources that are available • Timescales and deadlines imposed • The likely outcomes under alternative scenarios
Control	To control performance, management needs information to assess whether operations are proceeding as planned or whether there is some unexpected deviation from plan. If so, they may need to take some form of corrective action.
Performance measurement	Just as individual operations need to be controlled, so overall performance must be measured and reported, in a budgetary control report or a scorecard.
Decision making	Good-quality information should lead to better-informed decisions. The larger the organisation, the more robust the systems required. Lots of information will need to be processed and then organised in a way which makes it usable by management.

3.4.2 Types of information

Different types and quantities of information are required by managers for different purposes.

KEY TERM

Strategic information: Information that is used to plan the objectives of the company and assess whether the objectives are being met. Strategic information is longer term by nature and may include market intelligence and competitor analysis.

Tactical information: Information that is used to decide how the resources of the business should be deployed and to monitor how efficiently they are being used. Tactical information could include cash flow forecasts and working capital management.

Operational information: Information that is used to ensure that specific tasks are planned and carried out properly within an organisation. Operational information would consider matters such as cash receipts and payments, bank reconciliations and goods received and despatch notes.

3.4.3 Information requirements in different sectors

The information requirements of commercial companies are influenced by the need to make and monitor profit, but companies may not always need the same types of information. Here are some typical information requirements of a manufacturing company and a service sector company.

Manufacturing company

For manufacturers, the nature of the products they make will determine the information they find most important, but an awareness of issues such as changeover times for production lines, the number of common parts used, the diversity of the product range and quality will be their main focus alongside basic issues such as productivity and efficiency.

Information type	Examples of each type
Strategic	Future demand estimates New product development plans Competitor analysis
Tactical	Variance analysis Departmental accounts Inventory turnover
Operational	Production reject rate Materials and labour used Inventory levels

Service sector company

The challenge for the service sector is the absence of any real tangible outputs – however, like all companies, those offering a service are still generally customer and results oriented. As a consequence, the difference between service and other companies' information requirements has decreased. Businesses have realised that most of their activities can be measured, and many can be measured in similar ways, regardless of the business sector.

Information type	Examples of each type
Strategic	Forecast sales growth and market share Profitability Capital structure
Tactical	Resource utilisation such as average staff time charged out, number of customers per hairdresser and number of clients per operative Trends from customer satisfaction ratings
Operational	Staff timesheets Customer waiting time Individual customer feedback

Activity 7: Information types

CCC is a small retail business specialising in carpets and flooring. The management team has a background in this sector.

Consider some of the information that management would need to look at in more detail to help them plan future budgets or amend longer-term plans.

Required

Complete the table below, using the pre-seen scenario and considering the sort of information CCC would need to have at each level in order to grow and become more successful in their sector.

Information type	Examples relevant to CCC
Strategic	
Tactical	
Operational	

4 Ethical and sustainability reporting

Aside from profitability and cash flow, organisations are increasingly being assessed by internal and external stakeholders on their ethical and sustainability practices and policies.

There are various ways in which the organisation can report performance and more generally communicate with its stakeholders on these matters.

4.1 Mission statement

KEY TERM

> **Mission statement:** A statement of a company's main objective, and its purpose, strategy and values.

Mission statements are published for the benefit of employees and other stakeholders of the organisation. There is no standard format, but mission statements should generally be:

- **Brief** – to help ensure they are easy to understand and remember
- **Flexible** – to help accommodate change
- **Distinctive** – to make the organisation stand out

4.2 Corporate social responsibility (CSR) reporting

Increasingly, organisations are being assessed on how they are acting as 'good corporate citizens.'

KEY TERM

> **Corporate social responsibility reports:** Outline the objectives for ensuring the ethical, sustainable and moral aims and achievements of the organisation.

These corporate social responsibility (CSR) reports are usually included within the annual report, and discuss their policies in terms of **ethical**, **environmental**, **charitable** and **sustainability** factors. Larger companies must report on their social and environmental activities and sustainability impact via dedicated disclosures embedded within their financial statements under reporting frameworks such as the **IFRS Sustainability Disclosure Standards**. However, even smaller companies are also publicising their policies to differentiate themselves from competitors. Although the detailed content is outside of the syllabus, you will need to have an understanding of how ethical and sustainability information has an impact on stakeholders.

Real-life example: Jaguar Land Rover

Jaguar Land Rover (JLR) takes its corporate social responsibility reporting very seriously and aims to provide as much information as possible regarding its aims, its results to date, and where it sees that it can develop in the future.

- The company's website states: 'Our vision is to be proud creators of the most desirable brands, for the most discerning of clients' (Jaguar Land Rover, 2026).
- The company has a strategy called 'Reimagine' which is described as 'creating the JLR vision for our brands, our vehicles and our clients. It is about the electrification of Range Rover, Defender, and Discovery, and the renaissance of Jaguar as an all-electric brand' (Ibid, 2026).
- According to Reimagine, JLR is aiming to become a net zero business by 2039 with electrification across its 'entire footprint.' (This is across all of its operations, not just the cars that it produces.)
- The strategy will focus on the environmental, societal, and community impacts of the company.
- The company is aiming to operate ethically, responsibly and transparently, with a number of community initiatives – including the JLR Foundation.

During 2025, JLR experienced a cyber-attack that stopped production for a number of weeks. Coupled with an uncertain future in relation to the transition from petrol and diesel engines, JLR is facing challenges to be able to meet its social and environmental commitments but has nonetheless been clear in its strategic aims.

(**Source**: https://www.jlr.com/ [Accessed 23 February 2026])

4.3 Sustainability reporting

The following are examples of **responsibilities** for an organisation to uphold the principles of sustainability:

(a) Creating and promoting an **ethical culture** within the company:

  (i) Supporting ethical policies as they are introduced

  (ii) Discouraging and reporting illegal or unethical practices (money laundering, fraud, theft, bribery, non-compliance with regulations, bullying and short-term decision making)

(b) Championing the aims of **sustainability** within the context of the company's culture and its own policies on sustainability

(c) Evaluating and quantifying **reputational** and other **ethical risks**

(d) Taking **social**, **environmental** and **ethical factors** into account when preparing information for **decision-making** and **performance measurement**

(e) **Promoting sustainable practices** in relation to products and services, customers, employees, the workplace, the supply chain, and business functions and processes

(f) Raising awareness of **social responsibility**

4.4 Ethical reporting

Organisations may also have ethical **values**, based on the **norms** and **standards of behaviour** that their leaders believe will best help them express their identity and achieve their objectives. Often, the ethical values of the company are set out in its mission statement.

Setting standards is important as **organisations are responsible for their actions** and can be held **accountable** for the effects of their actions on people and society. Often these standards are not legally binding, rather they are guidelines for specific industries to ensure best practice.

As such individual organisations should **behave ethically** towards any employees, customers, suppliers and communities affected by the decisions and actions that they take.

The Groceries Supply Code of Practice (GSCOP) is not a legal requirement for supermarkets – however, it outlines and makes recommendations upon retailers regarding fair payment times, supply agreements and rules regarding deductions (including marketing, penalties and delays).

Supermarkets which perform poorly are likely to be questioned by shareholders at AGMs, receive bad publicity and, potentially, lose sales or contracts with suppliers.

Increasingly, large companies are disclosing their ethical treatment of suppliers in their annual reports.

Real-life example: Waitrose Ltd

In the extract below from the John Lewis Partnership annual report (2025), Waitrose confirms that it adheres to the Groceries Supply Code of Practice (GSCOP). The organisation also states that it has a specific committee to monitor the treatment of suppliers, and uses its audit and risk committee to monitor adherence to this.

> Both the Order and, in particular, the Code, regulate Waitrose's everyday trading relationships with our Grocery suppliers, ensuring that, as a Designated Retailer, we treat our suppliers fairly. [...] The desire to treat our suppliers fairly is also enshrined within the Partnership's Constitution and therefore is in keeping with the Partnership's general ethos. The Audit and Risk Committee (ARC) has responsibility for satisfying itself that the GSCOP governance framework and systems are appropriate and effective.

You can read the full report here:

https://www.johnlewispartnership.co.uk/~/media/Files/J/john-lewis/corp/documents/jlp-plc-ara-2024-25.pdf [Accessed 23 February 2026]

4.5 Integrated reporting

It is clear that many businesses need to report more than just figures and financial results in their annual reports. With over 70% of consumers stating that they will prefer to use the service of more ethical companies, and over a third stating that would be happy to pay more to ensure that the companies they use are ethical (PR Newswire, 2023), it is clear that reporting in a more 'holistic' manner is increasingly important for modern businesses.

Integrated reporting (sometimes referred to as IR) is a way of reporting **financial**, **ethical** and **sustainability factors**, usually including information on the welfare of staff, assistance to the local community and the business's impact on the environment.

You will not be expected to produce an integrated report in your assessment, but you should be aware that this is one of the ways that businesses can report performances, both with **financial** and **non-financial** parameters in their annual report.

Activity 8: Ethical and sustainability information

The following are some extracts from the directors' report contained in CCC's financial statements for the year ended 31 December 20X2, together with the company's mission statement.

CCC mission statement

Our mission is to provide an excellent level of service to all of our customers – and we endeavour to offer our customers a quality product at a competitive price.

We aim to act ethically towards our suppliers, customers and staff, ensuring the best in service and supporting diverse needs and requirements.

The environment is important to us and we aim to recycle wherever possible. We promise to remove all of the packaging from customers' premises, and dispose of this in an environmentally friendly way.

Extract from the directors' report as at 31 December 20X2

Revenue has increased year on year, but margins on the sale and fitting of carpets have been affected by challenging market conditions with larger national firms' aggressive price promises affecting what we can demand for our products and services.

We have recently introduced a vinyl reclamation scheme which can recycle the offcuts from vinyl rolls. The company recycles the offcuts into making traffic cones. A small charge is made for this – however, the scheme has reduced our non-recyclable waste costs.

Due to a new contract with Umteeko, we are looking to expand our stores across the south coast of England as this is proving to be a very popular product.

Required

Identify the following:

(1) Ethical information provided by the directors and the mission statement

(2) Sustainability information provided by the directors and the mission statement

(3) The stakeholders who are most likely to be interested in this information

Ethical information	Sustainability information	Stakeholder

Chapter summary

- An organisation has a range of stakeholders – internal (directors/managers, employees and owners) and external (lenders, suppliers, customers, government, environment, and the local community).
- Stakeholders have differing information needs, and organisations need to provide information that meets these needs.
- The company's statutory financial statements serve a number of purposes:
  - To identify profit or loss; to demonstrate the directors' stewardship
  - To comply with statute; to help shareholders evaluate their investment
  - To help lenders/suppliers determine the company's ability to pay on time
  - To help government/regulators determine the company's compliance with its regulatory obligations
  - To provide information about the company more widely
- Statutory financial statements comprise statements of a statement of profit or loss, a statement of financial position, a statement of changes in equity, and a statement of cash flows.
- Financial statements are not the only external reporting requirement. HMRC will need to ensure that the organisation is paying sufficient tax based on their profits for the period.
- Management accounts provide information to internal stakeholders so that they can make decisions on resourcing and manage the company's profitability and cash flow.
- Other internal forms of reporting include budgets and scorecards, which contain a mixture of financial and non-financial information.
- Types of management information which are required include strategic, operational and tactical. These vary according to industry.
- A range of ethical and sustainability-related forms of reporting now exist and present different stakeholders with a more rounded view of the organisation and its place in the world.

Activity answers

Activity 1: Internal stakeholders

Directors of CCC

- **Management accounts** to review the overall performance of the company
- **Aged receivables** and **payables reports** to ensure that payments are being made on time to suppliers and that monies due from customers is being collected on a timely basis

  This is necessary for cash flow management.
- **Margin analysis** on the products or types of products being sold, to verify whether lines should be continued or replaced

  Given that the market for carpet is being squeezed and CCC has the local market in the Umteeko range, consider whether the organisation should focus on that longer term.

If this information is not received, there is a **risk** that the company will not be able to react quickly enough to changes in the market. **Cash flow control** is vital in a small organisation; if peaks and troughs in cash flow are not correctly managed, the organisation may have to resort to expensive emergency overdrafts or may be unable to take advantage of any bulk order or early settlement discounts which suppliers may offer.

By reviewing the margins and relative profitability of the different types of products, CCC can **react** more quickly to the market conditions and ensure that they have enough inventory in their more popular lines. Currently, only two members of the fitting team are Umteeko trained which, given the popularity of the product and CCC's regional monopoly on the distribution, seems on the low side. CCC may be at risk of missing an opportunity to develop this line of business to replace its reduced turnover from more traditional floorings, such as carpets and tiles.

Warehouse manager

- **Inventory levels** – what items are in stock and what has not moved for a long time

  This inventory may need to be provided against or written off.
- **Sales forecast** – what inventory needs to be purchased to ensure that customers receive their products in a timely manner
- **Supplier delivery** and **purchases schedule** to ensure that inventory deliveries are as expected and can be verified to what has been ordered, and that there is sufficient room in the warehouse
- **Liaison with the operations team** to ensure that the **inventory will be available** when the fitters are booked in to fit the product

Without strict inventory controls, products may not be available when the fitters are booked in to deliver and fit the products. This will be a waste of resource (fitter time) and risks upsetting the customer who was expecting their carpet or flooring to be fitted on a set date.

Operations manager

- **Sales order information** to plan the fitters and delivery routes for the week/month ahead
- **Annual leave details** from human resources (HR) to avoid everyone going on holiday at the same time, especially staff with specific skills or training
- **Liaison with the warehouse team** to ensure that the **inventory will be available** when the fitters are booked in to fit the product, otherwise this may cause problems with customer relations in terms of expectation of delivery

Wages clerk

- Details of **new starters/leavers**
- Information on **pay rises** authorised by management
- **Overtime** information authorised by the operations manager, to ensure that overtime is correctly paid on time

- **Sales commission** information authorised by the sales manager, to ensure that all commission has been verified by the sales manager and paid in a timely manner
- **Annual leave** and **sickness details** authorised by department managers, to ensure that holiday pay is correctly allocated, and details of sickness (and any sick pay) are logged and monitored
- **Contracts** for all staff (to ensure pay is set at the correct level)
- **Cash flow information** to ensure that there is sufficient money to pay the staff

  If staff cannot be paid on time, there is a risk of employee discontent and losing skilled members of the workforce.

Activity 2: External stakeholders

Key external stakeholders for CCC are likely to include some or all of the following:

- **Customers**, to ensure that the company is solvent

  If they have a paid a deposit, for example, they have some security in CCC being able to supply their product.
- **Suppliers**, especially any significant or new suppliers who will be assessing CCC for creditworthiness

  It will be helpful for CCC's cash flow to be able to buy supplies on credit.
- The **government**, including HM Revenue & Customs (HMRC) for PAYE and corporation tax and the Registrar of Companies to ensure that the financial statements are filed on time
- **Lenders**, such as the bank

  Because CCC has an overdraft and a loan, the lender will monitor CCC's solvency to ensure it is able to pay off its debts.
- **Competitors** who access information about CCC, including the statutory financial statements from the Registrar of Companies

  For a small company like CCC, however, the information may be limited to a statement of financial position, and small companies like CCC would want to minimise the amount of information a competitor would be able to view, provided they adhere to financial reporting regulations.
- **Regulatory bodies** would also be interested in the performance of the organisation, and if a complaint is made against the company, there may be further enquiry by consumer groups and the media. Poor quality work may also result in negative reviews on social media.
- **Umteeko** would also have an interest in the performance of CCC. They will be keen to ensure that only trained fitters and approved adhesives are being used with its product. They would also want to view the company's overall performance, as Umteeko relies upon CCC for the sales of their product in the area. There is always a risk for CCC that poor performance on their part could mean that Umteeko decide to use another company to act as their local distributor.
- **Environmental pressure groups** may be interested in the sustainability of the products supplied by CCC (eg how long do they last and what happens to old flooring once it is no longer required).

Activity 3: Financial statements

As CCC is a small company, the **external reporting information available publicly** may be restricted to the **statement of financial position** and the notes and accounting policies. Nevertheless, this will be of use to the customers, suppliers and lenders as they will be able to verify the solvency of the company. However, this will only be at a certain point in the financial year (31 December) and will not give an up-to-date picture of the financial health of a company.

The bank may require further details – eg **management accounts** and **cash flow forecasts** – to verify that CCC can continue to pay its debts. This information would normally only be available to internal stakeholders. Additionally, there may be information related to specific **loan covenants** – eg a stated level of interest cover that must be contractually supplied to the lender.

HMRC will want a **detailed set of financial statements** (companies must now provide detailed financial statements that are not abridged for tax purposes). Again, this information is only produced once a year and is not a guarantee that the tax will be paid on time or whether the company will default on its payments.

HMRC also requires monthly information on the **payroll** (real-time information (RTI) reporting), which will ensure that payroll deductions are made correctly each month and the monies paid across in a timely manner.

Activity 4: Cash flows

The statement of cash flows separates out the net cash flows during the reporting period arising from:

- **Operating activities** – profit before tax for the period plus changes in current assets and liabilities excluding non-cash items

  Depreciation and finance costs are added back as these are not cash flows from the business so cash used in operating activities was actually a cash outflow of £14,000.
- **Movements in working capital** as represented by the increase or decrease in the balances for receivables, payables and inventories

  In this period, there was a net outflow of £30,000 represented by:
  - Inventory increasing by £24,000 – so CCC is holding more inventories
  - Trade receivables increasing by £51,000 as a result of higher sales on credit in the year
  - Trade payables increasing by £45,000 as a result of increased purchases to support higher sales and inventory levels
- After the interest paid of £5,000 is deducted (there was no tax paid), the net cash used in operating activities was £19,000.
- **Investing activities** (buying or disposing of non-current assets) so £2,000 was spent on new assets for use in the business.
- **Financing activities** – paying dividends, taking out or paying back loans, issuing new shares

  £60,000 was received from the new loan taken out during the year.
- All of the above cash flows are then reconciled to the **opening and closing cash positions** – the balance of the cash at hand less the overdraft. At the start of the year, there was a cash asset of £4,000 and a cash overdraft of £78,000, so a net cash position of (£74,000). The operating and investing activities of CCC have both result in net cash outflows during the year. However, the receipt of the £60,000 loan has improved the overall cash position during the year so there is a net increase in cash and cash equivalents of £39,000. At 31 December 20X2, there is a £2,000 cash asset and the overdraft has reduced to £37,000, a net cash position of (£35,000).
- The statement therefore summarises **where the business has generated its cash in the year**, and what it has **spent its cash on** in the period.

Activity 5: CCC budgetary control report

(a) Areas of focus

The sales team appear to be exceeding expectations by selling more Umteeko Oak (£1,750 favourable variance) and at a better price than budgeted (£975 favourable variance). However, Stefan should highlight the adverse variances in respect of material usage (£7,500) and labour efficiency (£4,250).

There may be issues with the budgetary process in calculating how much Umteeko Oak is required – for example, a customer may want a 25 m^2 room covered but this may require more than 25 m^2 of flooring depending on the shape of the room. From the analysis, the £7,500 adverse material usage variance indicates that either the fitters are using too much Umteeko Oak during the fitting process, or the budget itself is not allowing for realistic levels of wastage eg offcuts.

The £4,250 adverse labour efficiency variance may be related to this. The pre-seen information has highlighted an issue with the lack of fitting time allocated to the Umteeko product. The budget may need to be revised and the sales price amended upwards to reflect the additional time and procedures in fitting this specialist product.

(b) Limitations

The budgetary control report does not show the absorption of fixed costs, which is vital in terms of pricing, as the price charged must cover both fixed and variable costs if a business is to be profitable. If the fixed costs (eg rent) are not priced into the budgetary control report, then the directors will not fully understand why they are making losses or very small overall profits.

Only a certain number of products are currently being monitored due to the limitations of the system (Excel based) and the limited time, experience and judgement of Stefan.

By only selecting a few products, it does not help the directors to fully understand why CCC is struggling financially.

Activity 6: Balanced scorecard and ratios

The directors of CCC may wish to consider some of the following useful ratios and indicators for success to monitor the company's success in respect of the objectives set by John Cookridge.

(a) Financial success

Gross profit percentage = (gross profit ÷ revenue) × 100%

	Year to 31 December 20X2	Year to 31 December 20X1
Gross profit percentage	(403 ÷ 1,106) × 100% = 36.4%	(297 ÷ 930) × 100% = 31.9%
Carpets	(92 ÷ 379) × 100% = 24.3%	(143 ÷ 425) × 100% = 33.6%
Vinyl	(311 ÷ 727) × 100% = 42.2%	(154 ÷ 505) × 100% = 30.5%

The gross profit of CCC has increased year on year based upon the financial statements. Using the information available in the extract from the management accounts for the same periods, it is clear that the vinyl side of the business is more profitable. (For 20X2, carpets made a gross profit percentage of 24.3% compared to that of vinyl of 42.2%.) This is potentially down to the success of the Umteeko product. The profitability of vinyl has increased by approximately 13% since the prior year (which had no Umteeko business).

It would be useful for the directors to understand in more detail which product lines in the vinyl business are making the highest profits, and whether any of the carpet lines are unprofitable and need to be retired. This can only be analysed by a more detailed analysis of the profitability of each product line.

Another useful ratio which can be calculated is the operation profit percentage, calculated as (profit from operations ÷ revenue) × 100%, as this will reveal the extent to which the company is controlling its indirect costs.

(b) Customer satisfaction

Currently, CCC has no way of monitoring customer satisfaction (based on the information available). Recommended options may include:

- Analysing the number of repeat customers over a certain period
- Undertaking a customer satisfaction survey
- Logging the number of customer complaints and the nature of them (quality of product, fitting service and staff professionalism)

(c) Process efficiency

Cash flow can be monitored using a series of liquidity and working capital ratios.

For example:

		Year to 31 December 20X2	Year to 31 December 20X1
Trade payables payment period	(Trade payables ÷ cost of sales) × 365 days	(131 ÷ 703) × 365 = 68 days	(86 ÷ 633) × 365 = 50 days
Working capital cycle	Inventory holding period + trade receivables collection period – trade payables payment period	44 + 44 – 68 = 20 days (85 ÷ 703) × 365 = 44 days (134 ÷ 1,106) × 365 = 44 days (131 ÷ 703) × 365 = 68 days	35 + 33 – 50 = 18 days (61 ÷ 633) × 365 = 35 days (83 ÷ 930) × 365 = 33 days (86 ÷ 633) × 365 = 50 days
Quick ratio or 'acid test'	(Current assets less inventories) ÷ current liabilities	(134 + 2) ÷ (131 + 37 + 5) = 0.79:1	(83 + 4) ÷ (86 + 78 + 3) = 0.52:1

The **trade payables payment period** shows that CCC is taking much longer to pay its suppliers and, as these are over 68 days (most businesses offer terms of credit of around a month), this is a worrying sign and should flag up to the directors that there is a problem. It may be that the invoices are not being paid until CCC staff are chased for payment (which is not good for supplier relations and goes against the ethical treatment towards suppliers as set out in the company mission statement). CCC may lose credit status with suppliers and therefore have to pay for inventory up front – known as 'proforma invoicing' – or lose that supplier altogether. The directors will need to understand whether this is a systematic failure across the whole of accounts payable or whether just one or two large (and disputed) invoices are causing the ratio to be distorted.

The **working capital cycle** is short, which is good news, as it lowers the amount of money tied up in the business. However, below the headline figures there are potentially problems arising with the trade receivables – as these have increased from 33 to 44 days. Again, the directors need to focus on why this is happening, and what action should be taken to prevent a cash flow crisis.

The **quick ratio or 'acid test'** proves what the earlier two ratios have already highlighted. As the ratio is less than 1:1, it highlights that the current assets are not sufficient to pay the suppliers (or other current liabilities) at that current time. Although the ratio is improving, there are still significant issues for the directors to investigate.

(d) Growth

CCC should undertake an analysis of what training has been undertaken by its staff and consider whether this is sufficient for their needs. Only Stefan is undertaking any current accountancy training and there are only two Umteeko trained fitters. As CCC intends to use its success in the Umteeko product to expand its business, it should consider expanding the level of training to other fitters, especially those trained only on carpets, as this is a shrinking market.

Currently, CCC has no further data on what the competition is doing in terms of other local independent flooring companies. Analysis into the local competition and monitoring of the growth of national firms in the local area would aid CCC's strategic planning – especially if it is planning to open new stores in the region.

Activity 7: Information types

Information type	Examples relevant to CCC
Strategic	Forecast sales growth and market share Profitability of the different types of product lines (carpet vs vinyl) Capital structure and gearing analysis (the company is highly geared with the loan and overdraft) New stores to be opened in the region (who are the local competition? Does the local economy suit a high-quality flooring sold at a premium price, or should it have a discounted store to sell on discontinued lines/off-cuts?) Consideration of independent and national competitors (little point in setting up a store next to a large, heavy-discounting national competitor)
Tactical	Resource utilisation such as sales per sales team member Commission on a scale based on the type of product that CCC wants to focus on/launch new products, eg focusing on Umteeko products as they have better profit margins, so it makes tactical sense for the salespeople to focus on the products which have higher profit margins Material wastage by product (can the flooring be cut in a more economical manner to minimise waste off-cuts?) Trends from customer satisfaction ratings
Operational	Staff timesheets and monitoring of efficiency and utilisation (does every fitter manage to fit the same amount of flooring over a certain area, or are others better suited to more complex floorings?) Customer ordering to delivery time Individual customer feedback/customer satisfaction survey

Activity 8: Ethical and sustainability information

Ethical information	Sustainability information	Stakeholder
Mission statement stating CCC's intention to behave ethically towards its customers	Recycling information in the directors' report in the financial statements and the mission statement highlighting other recycling which is important to any customers who are seeking more sustainable suppliers. Looking to open new stores across the south coast of England, stating that the future is promising and the company is looking ahead to expand further in the region.	Customers

Ethical information	Sustainability information	Stakeholder
Mission statement stating CCC's intention to behave ethically towards its suppliers	Information regarding CCC's potential move away from carpets and towards vinyl (implicit in the directors' report) may signal to carpet suppliers to offer bigger discounts to CCC or attract other vinyl suppliers to approach CCC.	Suppliers
Mission statement stating that it supports diverse needs and behaves ethically towards its staff may attract new employees with physical or other disabilities to consider CCC when applying for employment	Information in the directors' report implies that the company is a going concern and expansion may offer additional opportunities to staff keen to develop their skills and experience within CCC.	Employees/potential employees
Some investors may want more information regarding the specific ethical actions of the business – eg some will invest in companies which recycle. The mission statement and directors' report both make statements to this effect at CCC.	Information in the directors' report implies, due to the expansion of stores, the contract with Umteeko and its aims to reduce costs that the company should be likely to continue for the foreseeable future. The information also demonstrates that management are aware of the limitations of the current market conditions and what they are doing to mitigate these risks.	Investors and potential investors

Test your learning

1 **Complete the following statement:**

A statement of cash flows shows receipt of a loan as part of [▼] and proceeds from the disposal of non-current assets as part of [▼] .

Picklist

- Financing activities
- Investing activities
- Operating activities

2 It is likely that all management decisions will have a financial or economic impact, but organisations also need to consider whether there are other impacts from the decisions made by management.

Required

From the options provided, identify the most likely additional impact on the organisation in each scenario.

	Ethical ✓	Environmental ✓
Improving recycling rates in the factory by 30% year on year		
Changing supplier who can supply the materials 20% cheaper, but with less control over the supply chain		
Installing a carbon capture unit on the main factory costing £2 million		
Introducing a more generous pension scheme for employees		

3 **Identify whether the following statements about stakeholders are true or false.**

	True	False
According to Mendelow's Matrix, stakeholders with high levels of power and low levels of interest should be kept informed.	○	○
Suppliers tend to want fair terms of trade with customers who display realistic prospects of success.	○	○
One example of an internal stakeholder is a shareholder.	○	○
Another example of an internal stakeholder is a lender.	○	○

4 You need to know about the various forms of external financial reporting. One such report can be described as follows:

'A reconciliation of opening and closing balances which enables stakeholders to see the impact of new share issues, profit or loss and dividends paid.'

Required

Which of the following external financial reports is being described?

	✓
Statement of financial position	
Statement of profit or loss	
Statement of changes in equity	
Statement of cash flows	

5 You need to know about the various forms of ethical and sustainability reporting that are important to both internal and external stakeholders.

Required

For each of the following descriptions, match them to the appropriate form of reporting.

Description	Type of report
A company's main objective, and its purpose, strategy and values	▼
The norms and standards of behaviour that express the organisation's identity and help it to achieve its objectives	▼
A way of reporting financial, ethical and sustainability factors	▼

Picklist

- Corporate social reporting
- Ethical reporting
- Integrated reporting
- Mission statement
- Stakeholder reporting
- Sustainability reporting

6 Organisations need varying types of information. The required level of information can be operational, tactical or strategic, depending on what is being monitored.

Required

For each of the following types of management information, identify the level that it is describing.

	Strategic	Tactical	Operational
A report produced by consultants that describes the technology infrastructure changes by industry in the next ten years	O	O	O
The individual feedback from one customer experience	O	O	O
Analysis of feedback from all customer experiences	O	O	O
The balance on the sales ledger	O	O	O

2 Internal control systems and fraud

Learning outcomes

2.1	**How internal controls can support the organisation** Students need to be able to: • Explain the purpose of internal controls • Assess how a strong system of internal controls can minimise the risk of loss to an organisation • Assess how a strong system of internal controls can ensure ethical standards in an organisation • Identify the types of internal controls used in different parts of the accounting function • Consider how different types of internal control suit different types of organisation
2.2	**Ways of preventing and detecting fraud and systemic weaknesses** Students need to know: • The common types of fraud • The common types of systemic weaknesses and their causes • The need for segregation of duties • The financial and non-financial implications for an organisation if fraud occurs • The role of internal controls in preventing fraud and errors • The role of internal controls in detecting fraud and errors
3.3	**The risk of fraud arising from weaknesses in the internal control system** Students need to be able to: • Identify the impact of a poor internal control system on the exposure to risk for an organisation • Grade the risk of fraud using either 'low, medium, or high' or a numerical grade where the number increases in size as the risk becomes more serious

Assessment context

The topics covered in this chapter are most likely to be included in Task 4 of the Role Scenario Assessment, which tests understanding internal control systems.

Qualification context

This chapter builds on content that you will have seen in your previous studies and will complement what you have learned at Level 4 in both Management Accounting and Financial Statements.

Business context

A system of internal control is designed to ensure the company does not fall prey to fraud or error, including misstatement of its financial statements. This ensures that the company can operate effectively. Every company's system is at risk of fraud and error even if the risk never actually materialises. A company with systemic weaknesses in its internal control system is particularly at risk. It can lead to serious losses and fines for the company, criminal prosecutions of those responsible, and ultimately the collapse of the company.

Chapter overview

Internal control systems and fraud

- Internal controls
- The control environment
- Types of control activities
- How a strong system of internal control can ensure ethical standards are met within an organisation
  - Limitations of a system of internal controls
- Internal control systems for different types of organisations
- What is fraud?
- Impact of fraud
  - What can cause fraud to occur?
- Controls to prevent fraud and systemic weaknesses
  - Sales system fraud
  - Purchases system fraud
- Detecting fraud
  - Management accounts
  - Ratio analysis
- The risk assessment process
- Fraud matrix
  - Identifying the grade of risk
- Monitoring controls

Introduction

In this chapter, we look at the purpose and type of internal controls commonly found in an organisation.

A strong system of internal control minimises financial loss within an organisation and can ensure that ethical standards are maintained.

Weak controls are one of the reasons that fraud may occur within an organisation. We will look at the common types of fraud and the implications of fraud within an organisation.

Organisations need to have good internal controls to prevent fraud taking place, with particular focus on the importance of the segregation of duties within the accounting function.

Accounting systems are at risk of specific frauds, namely payroll fraud, payables ledger fraud and receivables ledger fraud. We will look at the controls that should be in place to prevent these.

Management should assess the risk of fraud and misstatement for each area of the organisation, and we can see how fraud could be graded using a fraud matrix.

1 Internal controls

KEY TERM

> **Internal controls:** Policies and procedures that address the risk that the aims and objectives of the organisation will not be met.

The purpose of internal controls is to:

- Facilitate operations
- Safeguard assets
- Prevent and detect fraud
- Ensure quality of internal and external reporting
- Compliance

Internal controls work alongside the **control environment** to create the overall control framework. This is known as the **system of internal control**.

KEY TERM

> **System of internal control:** The control environment, the entity's risk assessment process, the entity's processes to monitor the system of internal control, the information system and communication and control activities.
>
> **Systemic weaknesses:** Weaknesses that arise within the accounting system itself, which leave it open to fraud and error.

Robust systems of internal controls:

- Reduce systemic weaknesses in the accounting system, including the scope for errors
- Reduce the risk of loss or fraud
- Ensure that the accounting system operates appropriately
- Ensure the accounting system can change in line with the environment and organisational requirements
- Ensure that ethical standards are met within an organisation

2 The control environment

KEY TERM

> **Control environment:** Formed by the attitudes, awareness and actions of management and those responsible for ensuring that the internal controls within the organisation meet its needs.

The control environment is part of the system of internal controls, alongside the internal controls themselves.

The owners or management of an organisation must ensure that these control activities are **regularly monitored** to ensure that nothing goes wrong. If the controls are not followed and management do nothing in response, the system of internal controls will not operate effectively – eg if a manager knowingly authorises a fraudulent expense claim by a subordinate, the internal control requiring expenses to be authorised by management is undermined by the weak control environment.

Management must regularly assess the **existing** system and **identify any new risks** which may affect how robust the control system currently is. Without this monitoring, there is unlikely to be a strong control environment.

Indications of a good control environment include the following:

(a) Management communicate and enforce integrity and ethical behaviour.

(b) Management and staff are well trained and competent.

(c) Management operates in a way that promotes control – eg regularly monitoring whether the controls are working and adhered to in practice.

(d) The company and accounting function is structured in a way that promotes control.

(e) Authority and responsibility for controls is assigned to separate people – ie segregation of duties is commonplace.

(f) Human resources (HR) policies promote controls.

(g) Management regularly review and reassess any new or potential risks to assess whether the controls in place are robust enough to ensure a strong control environment.

3 Types of control activity

KEY TERM

> **Control activities:** Policies and procedures that help ensure that objectives are carried out.
>
> **Segregation of duties:** Making sure that a number of people are involved in different parts of each process to minimise the opportunity for fraud and error.
>
> **Physical controls:** Ensuring assets (eg inventory and cash) are safe via the use of locked doors, security cameras and inspections.

The types of control activity that should be used in an accounting system to address systemic weaknesses can be remembered using the mnemonic **SPAMSOAP**:

(a) **S**egregation of duties – eg different members of staff should (i) open the post, (ii) record any cash or cheques received, and (iii) bank cash and cheques received. These can be built into integrated computer systems (eg an invoice is raised by one user) but a manager must log in to approve them. Others may be manual, such as proof of authorisation by a signature on a hard copy report.

(b) **P**hysical controls – controls over the physical security of accounting records and assets such as cash and inventory – eg lock cash receipts in a safe until they are banked; require codes to unlock the cash tills; lock the locations where inventory is kept.

(c) **A**uthorisation controls

KEY TERM

> **Authorisation and approval of transactions:** Undertaken by supervisors and managers. This shows the person processing the transaction that it is valid – eg overtime should be approved by departmental heads.
>
> **Authorisation controls:** These ensure that only authorised personnel can make changes, such as to standing data or to authorise a bank payment.

(d) **M**anagement controls – managers should review whether activity controls are being carried out within the accounting system, eg comparing budget to actual performance in a budgetary control report, and comparing performance and position from one period to the next using ratio analysis.

(e) **S**upervision controls – there should be close oversight of people performing accounting tasks day to day.

KEY TERM

> **Reviews:** Performed by supervisors or managers by looking at summaries and reports of transactions – eg to ensure they are reasonable.

(f) **O**rganisation – the way tasks and the business as a whole are organised should support internal control – eg clear lines of responsibility, cover, delegation and reporting, and adequate resources being available for the accounting system.

(g) **A**rithmetic and accounting controls – checks on whether transactions have been processed accurately and completely – eg **reconciliations** such as a bank statement and a cash book, or a payables ledger account and a statement from the supplier, can also highlight if errors have occurred.

KEY TERM

> **Accounting controls:** Controls which help to identify mistakes in the accounting records.

Other accounting controls can be highlighted by a trial balance being out of balance or a computer system not allowing a journal to be posted where the debits do not equal the credits.

KEY TERM

Reconciliations: Controls that check whether two different sources of information agree or that any differences are understood – eg bank reconciliations verifying the bank statement to the bank account on the nominal ledger.

(h) **P**ersonnel controls – appropriately recruited, selected and trained accounting staff should be employed.

Activity 1: The control environment

Consider the following scenario at CCC which occurred in September 20X2:

Stefan was the first to arrive at work on Monday morning. He opened the post, and began logging cash and cheques received into the day book when the telephone rang. It was Margaret to say that she had an emergency dental appointment for that morning, so she would be late for work. Stefan went back to his task of processing the mail; without noticing he had dropped a cheque behind the desk, before he had written it into the day book. Stefan put the day book, with the cheques inside, onto his desk whilst he went to discuss the morning's deliveries with the warehouse manager.

Paula Cookridge popped into the office before she joined her husband, John, for lunch. As she was short on cash and did not have time to go to the bank, she helped herself to £40 from the petty cash tin, and told Stefan that John would replace it this afternoon when he returned from their lunch date.

Paul Collins asked when Pritpal, one of the fitters, would be at work as he needed some rolls of vinyl to be moved into the warehouse from the pallet delivery outside. Pritpal is certified in counter-balance forklift truck operation. In Pritpal's absence, Jake Brew offered to move the vinyl as he has been shown how to use the forklift by Pritpal on a number of occasions. Paul accepts his offer as Pritpal is delayed in traffic.

John was concerned that some customers were becoming increasingly slow in making payments on their credit accounts. He asked Stefan to prepare a schedule of receivables, but Stefan was busy drawing up the sales invoices (he uses his Word template and manually inputs details from the sales team) and asked if this could be done next month. Stefan had not chased up late payments recently because he was too busy. Constructing a receivables ledger from the Word document invoices took at least two to three hours, and there was a lot of post still to be processed that morning.

Sonja, who had been on holiday, was approached by Ron Sellers, one of the sales team. He had been expecting commission totalling £800 in his wages, but Margaret (who had covered for Sonja last month) had not processed this and had only prepared his wages based on Ron's basic hours worked. Ron told Sonja that he really needed this money, but Sonja, knowing she could do nothing until the next wages run, told Ron he would have to wait seven days.

Ron was so upset by this news that Sonja was consumed with guilt, and she told Ron that she would borrow the money out of the petty cash tin and replace it when she made his wages up next week.

Margaret keeps the company cheque book in her drawer, but as she only works part time, the drawer is often left unlocked.

Required

Highlight areas of weakness from the extract above relating to CCC.

4 How a strong system of internal control can ensure ethical standards are met within an organisation

KEY TERM

> **Ethics:** A set of generally accepted principles that guide behaviour.
>
> **Ethical values:** Assumptions and beliefs about what constitutes 'right' and 'wrong' behaviour.
>
> **Fundamental principles of professional ethics:** The principles that underpin how a professional accountant should behave.

Individuals hold ethical values, often reflecting the beliefs of the families, cultures and educational environments in which they grew up. Sometimes, these are referred to as **ethical standards**.

Companies should also have ethical values, based on the **norms** and **standards of behaviour** that their leaders believe will best help them express their identity and achieve their objectives. The values of the company are usually set out in its **mission statement** but may also be demonstrated in other ways.

Companies, just like individuals, are members of society and are therefore **responsible for their actions**, and can be held accountable for the effects of those actions – eg companies can be convicted of crimes such as manslaughter, just like people.

Therefore, companies should behave ethically towards their stakeholders.

You will have met the **fundamental ethical principles** earlier in your studies - they are defined in the AAT *Code of Professional Ethics* (the AAT Code) as follows:

KEY TERM

Integrity: Being straightforward and honest in all professional and business relationships.

Objectivity: Not allowing bias, conflict of interest or undue influence of others to override professional or business relationships.

Professional competence and due care: Having the right level of current professional knowledge and skill to give competent professional service, and acting diligently and in accordance with applicable and professional standards.

Confidentiality: Not disclosing confidential information except in appropriate circumstances, and not profiting from confidential information.

Professional behaviour: Complying with relevant laws and regulations and not bringing disrepute on the accounting profession (AAT, 2024).

Activity 2: Internal controls and ethical standards

We have already seen how the control environment can support the adoption of ethical behaviour in an organisation.

Required

Using examples from CCC to illustrate your answer, describe how a system of internal control can support the achievement of ethical standards.

4.1 Limitations of a system of internal controls

No system is perfect. The inherent limitations of a system of internal controls could include the following:

- People make mistakes that may not be picked up by software or human review (**human error**).
- People may not realise they are **operating controls incorrectly**, rendering them redundant.
- People may deliberately **circumvent** control systems if they want to defraud the company, either individually, or by colluding together.
- **Lack of review** of the controls in place (and any punitive action for non-compliance) means that there is no incentive for staff to follow them.

- An overreliance on controls, especially computerised controls, can breed **complacency** meaning they go undetected.
- The perfect control may be **too expensive** to implement, meaning that compromises are made and systems are flawed.

Assessment focus point

If you are asked in the assessment to consider the limitations of controls, ensure you have read the scenario carefully to ensure your answer is tailored to the question – eg in the case of CCC, there appears to be little or no regular review of the controls. Stefan is asked about the aged receivables report when cash flow becomes an issue rather than on a regular, monthly timetable.

5 Internal control systems for different types of organisation

As regulation and reporting requirements become more complex, the underlying system of internal controls must also be reviewed and assessed for suitability by management.

The level of complexity and size of the system of internal controls will depend on the size and nature of the organisation.

Large companies produce significant amounts of data which is usually recorded electronically. Therefore, large companies usually need a mixture of controls over electronic data as well as some manual internal controls. Large companies usually have lots of staff which makes segregation of duties easier.

A **small or medium-sized company** may have fewer staff members to perform controls and therefore they are less able to implement segregation of duties. These companies might use simpler accounting systems with more manual controls.

Businesses that are **cash-based** should have good physical controls over cash and regular reconciliations to ensure that the cash balances are correct, for example reconciling the cash register balance at the end of the day. A cash-based business is usually considered to be riskier than a business that operates on credit.

Credit-based businesses tend to have a lot more documentation at each stage of their transaction cycles. This paper (or electronic) documentation makes it easier to establish an audit trail to implement internal controls and monitor whether they have been adhered to.

Online businesses will need different controls to physical businesses. As well as strong controls over the IT systems, there will need to be good physical controls over any inventory, especially as these businesses often have higher levels of returns.

6 What is fraud?

You were introduced to the concept of fraud and the regulations surrounding it earlier in your studies. It is useful to review the key points before attempting the activities in this section.

KEY TERM

Fraud: A deliberate or intentional act to gain some form of advantage, or to cause loss to another party, from the use of deception.

Legally, there are three types of fraud (Fraud Act 2006: s. 1):

- False representation
- Failure to disclose information
- Abuse of position

With respect to the accounting system, the types of fraud which are important are:

KEY TERM

> **Misappropriation of assets:** Theft, teeming and lading, payment of false employees/suppliers.
>
> **Misstatement of the financial statements:** The overstatement of assets or profit, or the understatement of profit, losses or liabilities.

An accounting system is more open to fraud if it contains systemic weaknesses, making it easy to misappropriate assets, or misstate financial information.

Examples of fraud include, but are not restricted to:

- Falsifying financial statements or documents, eg invoices
- Incorrect accounting to purposely hide debts or overstate profits
- False claims about the products being sold by the company (eg Silicon Valley start-up Theranos)
- Payment fraud, including teeming and lading (misallocation of cash payments)
- Tax evasion – eg understatement of VAT, PAYE or corporation tax
- Money laundering
- Insider trading
- Embezzlement (fraud by employees in positions of power or trust within a business), such as by creating fictitious suppliers or employees

Activity 3: Potential frauds at CCC

Using the information obtained about CCC from the pre-seen information and any existing knowledge about CCC, consider the key areas where fraud may occur within the business.

Required

Identify the possible frauds that could occur within CCC – even if the controls currently in place make such a fraud unlikely.

	Potential fraud
Purchases and inventory system	
Payroll system	
Bank and cash system	
Sales and aged receivables system	

7 Impact of fraud

Fraud has the following types of impact on a company:

(a) **Financial** – loss of funds or other assets. This in turn affects the company's profitability and the owner's investment in it. It can also affect the company's share price.

(b) **Reputation** – exposure to fraud can affect the company's reputation in the eyes of internal and external stakeholders. This in turn could lead to a loss of business.

(c) **Employee morale** – the trust of existing employees could be damaged. Future recruitment and retention of staff might also be affected.

The following examples illustrate the financial and reputational impacts upon companies which have been fined for financial misstatement, or not having sufficient fraud prevention controls in place:

Real-life example: Tesco Stores

In March 2017, Tesco Stores was fined £129 million by the Serious Fraud Office (SFO) and ordered to set up an £85 million compensatory scheme for shareholders and bondholders who bought shares between the results announcement and the accounting misstatement being made public. Tesco settled out of court regarding charges of false accounting and misstatement of profits.

The impact on the company was a £214 million cash outflow, not including legal costs, with Tesco recording an exceptional charge of £235 million for the 2016/2017 accounting year end.

(**Source**: https://www.reuters.com/article/uk-britain-tesco-fraud-idUKKBN16Z0KD [Accessed 26 February 2026])

Real-life example: Rolls-Royce plc

Rolls-Royce plc was fined £497.5 million by the SFO in January 2017 in respect of 12 counts of conspiracy to corrupt, false accounting and failure to prevent bribery over a period of 30 years. In addition, the company was fined $170 million by to the US Department of Justice and $25 million by the Brazilian authorities.

(**Source**: https://www.rolls-royce.com/media/press-releases/2017/17-01-2017-statement.aspx [Accessed 26 February 2026])

Real-life example: NatWest Bank

The Financial Conduct Authority (FCA) fined the National Westminster (NatWest) Bank £264.8 million for three offences of failing to comply with money laundering regulations regarding the activity of a commercial customer between November 2012 and June 2016.

When originally taken on by the bank, Fowler Oldfield, a Bradford-based jewellery business, was not expected to deal in cash, but deposited around £365 million (including £264 million in cash) over the period in question. This activity was later confirmed to involve large-scale money laundering The fine was levied because, although the bank identified several red flags (including significant amounts of Scottish bank notes that would not have been typical for an English business, plus other concerns that were raised when cash was deposited at NatWest branches), no action was taken, allowing the money laundering to continue.

(**Source**: https://www.fca.org.uk/news/press-releases/natwest-fined-264.8million-anti-money-laundering-failures [Accessed 26 February 2026])

7.1 What can cause fraud to occur?

Cressey (1973) explains that fraud is likely to occur if three conditions are present:

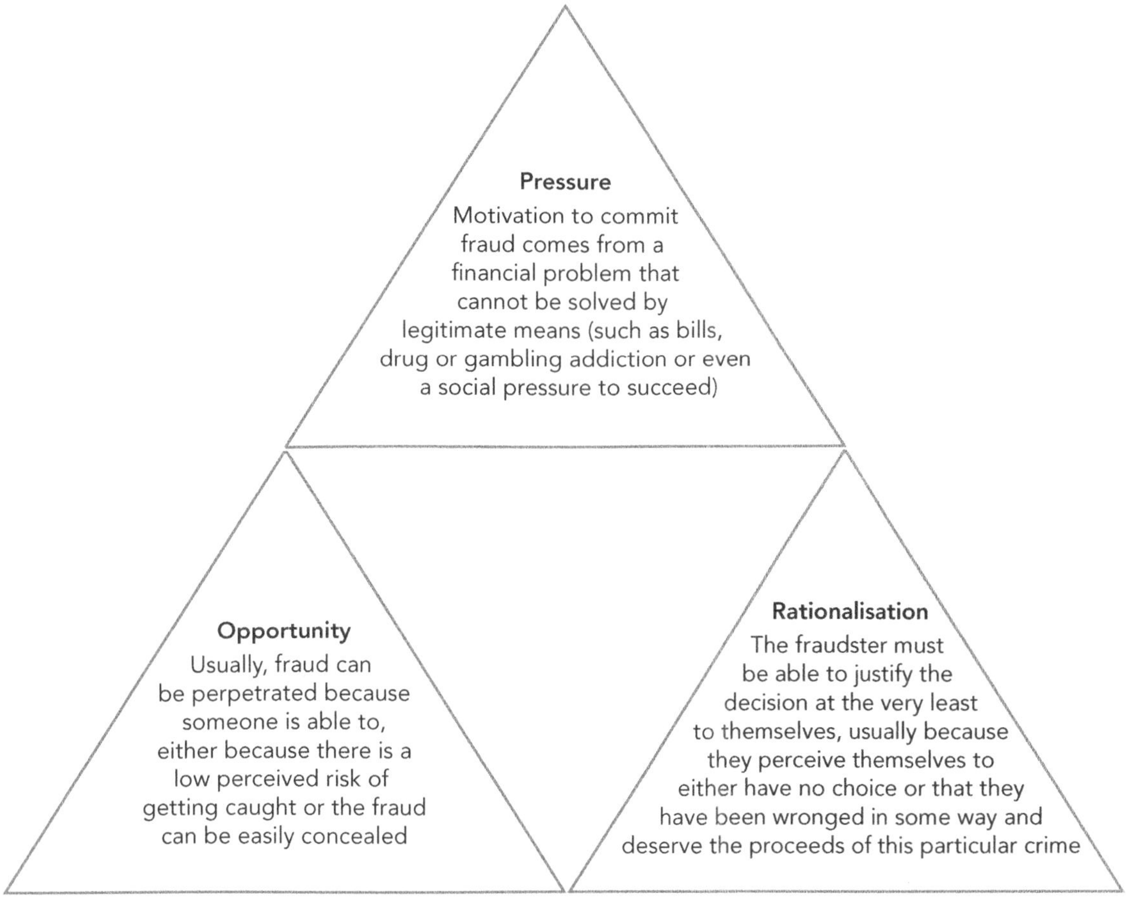

Figure 2.1: Fraud triangle

Knowing that fraud is usually a product of these three conditions means that an organisation can focus on each one when considering both **prevention** and **detection** of fraud. For example:

- **Pressure** – are staff likely to be affected by external factors (eg blackmail, addiction or extortion)?
- **Opportunity** – are assets likely to be vulnerable (and are any of our internal controls poor)?
- **Rationalisation** – are staff disenfranchised or desperate enough to commit fraud, and do our recruitment procedures always check employee references for any previous fraudulent behaviour?

Having a better understanding of the conditions that need to be present for fraud to occur can help an organisation design **suitable controls** that can attempt to **address** such conditions. The fraud triangle is a good way of understanding these conditions.

8 Controls to prevent fraud and systemic weaknesses

In this section, we look specifically at the types of fraud which can occur within the business and, using the scenario of CCC, identify potential issues and consider the impact on CCC.

The management of a company has a duty to put in place adequate controls to safeguard the company and its assets. You have seen many of the safeguarding controls earlier in your studies and have also covered them in this chapter (SPAMSOAP).

The main types of control which can help prevent fraud include controls for the accounting system. These can be grouped into the following categories:

- **Staff controls** – segregation of duties
- **Management controls** – regular reviews of controls and control activities
- **Physical controls** – locking away confidential files and ensuring office security
- **Information processing and generalIT controls** – password protection, access limitations and integration of systems

KEY TERM

> **Fraud controls:** Internal controls specifically against fraud in the areas of staff controls, management controls, physical controls and IT controls.

8.1 Sales system fraud

Fraud within the sales system is possible because the system involves the receipt of money, and this risk is more severe where this is in the form of cash.

Activity 4: Sales system fraud

The following is some further information given about an event in January 20X3 at CCC. Use this additional information and any existing knowledge about CCC to formulate your answer.

> Stefan was tidying up in the office one evening and was surprised to discover two cheques behind a desk. One was dated August 20X2, and one November 20X2. He put them in the in-tray intending to bank them the next day.
>
> John Cookridge asked for a copy of the aged receivables report, as he hadn't seen one for nearly four months. He was annoyed when he discovered that one of the credit accounts, opened for B. Braithwaite, had made no payments at all against credit given so far. This customer had bought £1,000 worth of goods and paid an initial deposit in July 20X2 but had made no payment since then. He asked Stefan to track back through the account and Stefan realised that no credit reference agency had been used to vet the customer before accepting their initial order, so he decided to contact the agency to check on this customer, only to find that they had a very poor credit score.
>
> Meanwhile John continued to review the aged receivables report and discovered that not only had debts been written off without his knowledge but also that over 50% of the invoices over 60 days old had no payments allocated against them. Unallocated cash amounted to £5,645.
>
> Stefan advised that there had been a large debt of £2,300 written off the previous month, as it dated back to the previous October. Stefan said that, although he had tried to chase the debt, the telephone number rang out, and the customer had taken the flooring with him (so no delivery address had been logged by the sales staff).
>
> When John came to lock up the business at the end of Thursday, he discovered that the tills on the shop floor had not been emptied or reconciled to the day's takings.

Required

(a) Identify the types of fraud which could occur in the sales system at CCC based on the information you have been given in this extract. You should also explain why you think this fraud risk has arisen.

Fraud which could occur at CCC	Why this risk has arisen

(b) Consider the financial and non-financial impacts these frauds could have on CCC.

8.2 Purchases system fraud

Fraud within the purchases system is possible because the system includes the ability to order goods from suppliers and then to make payments using the company's bank account.

One of the general controls in place to prevent such examples of fraud is segregation of duties. The same member of the accounting team should not be allowed to place orders with suppliers, book in goods received, and then process payments made to them.

Activity 5: Purchases system fraud

The following events happened at CCC during March 20X3:

> Margaret needed to place a stationery order for CCC. She asked the staff what they needed and placed the order, including some additional paper for her nephew who is studying at university.
>
> CarPet Suppliers, one of CCC's major suppliers, has requested urgent payment of an invoice that has been outstanding for 60 days. This invoice is for £15,000 and, though this would normally have been paid, there were not enough funds in the bank to cover this amount.
>
> When Margaret informed John of this, he was very surprised at the size of the invoice and asked her to review all the goods received notes (GRNs) for October to see what carpets had been ordered to cause such a large invoice. Margaret spent a day completing this reconciliation and found that there was an error and they had been charged for 1,000 metres of twisted Wilton instead of 100, this having a wholesale price of £15.00 per metre including VAT.
>
> When John was reviewing the invoice, he asked Margaret to produce a report of outstanding invoices and discovered some new suppliers with long outstanding debts which he did not recognise.

Required

Identify the risks from the control weaknesses in the above extract and make any recommendations to improve the controls.

Ensure your answer is specific to the scenario.

9 Detecting fraud

Internal controls within the accounting system should be designed not only to address weaknesses and prevent fraud and errors, but also to help detect when they have occurred.

The key controls that detect whether fraud or errors have occurred are:

(a) **Spot checks** on whether control activities have taken place

(b) **Performance reviews** and comparisons, using:

 (i) The **budgetary control report** – compare actual results to budgeted results.

 (ii) **Ratio analysis** – compare this period to the previous period, and evaluate the relationships between figures in the financial statements (eg level of receivables compared with level of sales).

(c) **Reconciliation** of information produced by the accounting system with external evidence, such as bank statements and supplier statements

(d) **Control accountreconciliations** where transactions are recorded in individual accounts and in total (eg receivables and payables)

Management can use financial information to analyse and review the controls of an organisation. Financial information can highlight issues such as potential inefficiencies as well as possible fraudulent behaviour, eg decreases in profit margin may suggest that costs are being poorly managed, or may highlight an issue such as theft of inventory.

9.1 Management accounts

Management reports can be structured to ensure that the most useful information is available to the user of the report. The information may be summarised into a form of profit or loss statement, or include additional information such as variance analysis, aged receivables analysis or capital expenditure review for the period.

Ideally, these reports should be consistently prepared and monitored on a regular basis, eg monthly, so as to highlight any significant issues arising, and to prompt investigations and corrective action where required.

Activity 6: Detecting fraud using financial information

The following are some extracts from the management accounts which were completed at the year end for CCC. Use these and the financial statements in the pre-seen scenario for this activity. CCC completes quarterly management accounts only.

Extracts from the management accounts for CCC Ltd as at 31 December 20X2

	20X2		20X1	
	Carpets	Vinyl	Carpets	Vinyl
	£'000	£'000	£'000	£'000
Revenue	379	727	425	505
Cost of sales	(287)	(416)	(282)	(351)
Gross margin	92	311	143	154

	All products		All products	
	£'000	£'000	£'000	£'000
Rent and rates	30		30	
Salaries: Administration and management	87		87	
Salaries: Sales	105		60	
Salaries: directors	120		110	
Motor expenses	19		10	
Irrecoverable debts	22		8	
Finance costs	5		6	
Other costs	13		10	
Total costs		401		321
Net profit/(loss)		2		(24)

Required

Using the knowledge you have obtained from the earlier activities, review the management accounts above and highlight areas which present potential issues for the company, making any recommendations you believe are appropriate.

Note. **There is no requirement to calculate ratios.**

9.2 Ratio analysis

A key way in which statutory financial statements are analysed by both internal and external stakeholders is the application of **ratio analysis**.

Ratio analysis is making **comparisons** between figures in a company's financial statements and how they **relate** to each other in order to determine the financial performance and position of the company. They can also be used as a way of identifying fraud from results that are otherwise **inconsistent** with your understanding of an entity.

The mechanics of how ratios are calculated are covered in Level 4 Financial Statements so are not covered in detail here, but you will be required to demonstrate your knowledge and application in this area within the role scenario assessment.

10 The risk assessment process

KEY TERM

> **Risk assessment process:** This includes the following: identify the risk; evaluate the risk; respond to the risk (manage/mitigate risk by taking appropriate action); ensure compliance (legal and regulatory); monitor, review and report.

As discussed earlier, management should **regularly review** the controls that are in place. Any review should include an assessment of any new risks, internal (eg a new computer system or management restructure) and external (increased market competition, issues with suppliers etc) that may impact the organisation. In doing so, any review should assess the ability of the internal control system to respond to the risk that:

(a) Objectives might not be met – including the company's sustainability and corporate social responsibility (CSR) objectives (eg sales targets, waste disposal, staff training requirements and recruitment concerns);

(b) The company may be the victim of loss or fraud – can be accidental or intended, and arise from internal or external sources;

(c) The system may contain errors that result in misstatement in the financial statements – eg assets overvalued and/or liabilities understated;

(d) The company is engaged in unethical behaviour – either intentionally (eg due to pressures to achieve unrealistic sales targets) or unintentionally (eg poorly trained staff taking on new tasks); and

(e) The company fails to comply with its legal obligations – eg non-compliance with company law or health and safety regulations.

The risk assessment process must be robust to reduce or avoid these risks. The main aim of analysing the risk of fraud is assessing the likelihood on the fraud occurring and its impact if it does occur and seeking out ways to minimise the risk.

KEY TERM

> **Risk of fraud:** The likelihood of the fraud occurring and its impact if it does occur.

Activity 7: Payroll risks

The following is some additional information on CCC regarding an event during October 20X2. You may also wish to refer to information given earlier in this chapter.

> Sonja, the payroll clerk, was approached once again by Ron Sellers, one of the sales team. He had been expecting commission totalling £1,200 in his wages for October but complained to Sonja that this had not correctly calculated and subsequently he had been underpaid. Ron was cross and aggressively told Sonja that he really needed the missing money right now.
>
> Sonja was so upset by this that she told Ron that she would borrow the money out of the petty cash tin and replace it when she made his wages up. Ron calmed down and said he would collect it from her at the end of the day and stated that he hoped it 'wouldn't happen again'.
>
> Joe Bloggins spoke to Sonja and explained that he had taken on an extra member of staff for the Christmas rush and January sales. Joe said that the new employee would be paid on an hourly basis, and that as he was a student, he would not pay tax and could be paid weekly in cash. Sonja asked for the new starter document that all new employees had to complete, but Joe insisted this was not necessary for temporary staff, and insisted Sonja just add him to the payroll system. Joe said that he would send through the completed document later in the week. Sonja agreed, and added the new worker, Andrew Lias, to the payroll, leaving herself a diary note to ask Joe for the documentation the next week if it was still outstanding.

Sonja's day was made even worse by the printer jamming, resulting in several of the payslips being printed upside down. Sonja was so fed up, she screwed the partially torn and smudged payslips into a ball and threw them in the bin, assured the directors that she would re-run the payslips first thing the next day, and went home early.

Required

Prepare a risk assessment summary for the payroll system for the directors of CCC. Highlight the key issues which have occurred in the payroll system during October and what regulatory and ethical risks these pose to the organisation.

To: The directors of CCC
Risk assessment of the payroll system based on events in October 20X2

11 Fraud matrix

KEY TERM

Fraud matrix: A map of the potential frauds against an organisation, cross-referenced to the risks of each of these occurring, documenting the controls over these risks. Also known as a risk matrix.

A fraud matrix helps the company:

- Investigate the **potential** for fraud within a system
- Analyse the **controls** currently in place to prevent fraud
- **Grade the potential** for fraud, according to risk

Although this approach is subjective, it enables a risk-based approach to improving controls that are appropriate to the company.

The risk to the company is graded on an appropriate scale, either numerically on a scale of 1–5 or by stating the deemed level of risk.

- 1 = low
- 3 = medium
- 5 = high

Possible improvements to the controls for all high and/or medium risks can then be recommended.

11.1 Identifying the grade of risk

The level of risk of fraud in a particular situation is graded as high, medium or low by identifying two factors:

- The **likelihood** of the risk occurring; and
- The potential **impact** of that risk on the company.

Illustration 1: CCC

In looking at the potential for the misappropriation of petty cash in CCC:

- The likelihood is high (5). Loose cash is easy to steal and it presents a strong temptation (especially in small amounts) as the person stealing it may not perceive the loss to be that 'bad' a thing for the company.
- The impact on the company is medium (3), as the company could potentially lose £1,200.

Combining these two factors, the overall risk of fraud in relation to petty cash would probably be graded as medium/high (4).

Activity 8: Fraud matrix CCC

Using your knowledge obtained to date of CCC, answer the following questions. (Use the table given to guide your answer.)

Required

Complete the fraud matrix below in respect of CCC. In particular you should:

(1) Identify four risks to CCC which may not be prevented or detected by the existing controls currently in place.

(2) Identify any regulation or law which could be broken by CCC as a result of these risks and the possible impact on the organisation.

Potential fraud	Controls currently in place	Risk to CCC 1 = low 5 = high	Implications/ regulations affected
1			
2			

Potential fraud	Controls currently in place	Risk to CCC 1 = low 5 = high	Implications/ regulations affected
3			
4			

12 Monitoring controls

Controls must be monitored to assess their effectiveness over time.

This review is usually overseen by management or, in larger organisations, an independent internal audit team. **Internal auditors** will review controls across different departments within the company. The role of internal audit differs from that of the external audit. The **external auditors** review the year-end financial statements and give an opinion as to whether the statements represent a true and fair view of the company.

Occasionally, both sets of auditors will work alongside each other, such as when the external auditors are assessing the controls within an IT system. However, it is important to note that whilst internal auditors are employed by the organisation, the external auditors are not. External auditors are typically engaged to assess the financial records on behalf of a company's shareholders for legal compliance purposes.

In **smaller organisations**, effective monitoring can take place, formally or informally, by function heads. For example, the sales director is likely to become aware of control deficiencies in the sales cycle, as they are responsible for managing the sales department's ongoing performance, so will investigate any reasons behind poor performance.

Assessment focus point

For the assessment, you may be expected to propose **monitoring**, **review** and **report** actions in response to an identified risk. It is important that you can define these terms in order to be able to apply them to a scenario.

KEY TERM

Monitoring, review and report: In this context, **monitoring** means looking at activity or behaviour related to a specified fraud risk because you need to know the extent of this activity or behaviour.

Review means gathering evidence of this activity or behaviour to understand the extent of this fraud risk.

Report means what you communicate to those higher up in the organisation as part of the overall risk management process.

Illustration 2: Monitoring, review and report at CCC

The fraud matrix that was completed for CCC included a number of fraud risks. For example:

- Overstatement of wages - additional cash being paid to staff for work not done
- Theft of inventory from the warehouse
- Writing off customer debts without authorisation

Required

How would you monitor, review and report on these fraud risks?

Fraud risk	Monitoring (activity/behaviour)	Review (evidence to collect)	Report (what gets communicated)
Overstatement of wages – additional cash being paid to staff for work not done			
Theft of inventory from the warehouse			
Writing off customer debts without authorisation			

Solution

Fraud risk	Monitoring (activity/behaviour)	Review (evidence to collect)	Report (what gets communicated)
Overstatement of wages – additional cash being paid to staff for work not done	Budget overspend or adverse variance Payments outside of contracted terms	Comparison of contract rates with actual payments Reconciliation of wage rates to employees' contracts of employment	Amount of any wage overspend by cause (not due to overtime or prior period error)
Theft of inventory from the warehouse	Inventory recorded as received but unable to be found when required	Instances of inventory leaving the warehouse without a legitimate reason (eg valid sales order)	Amount of inventory moved without legitimate documentation
Writing off customer debts without authorisation	Sales that are cancelled by staff without the appropriate authority	Sales written off without appropriate supporting documentation (eg credit note or journal approved by a senior member of staff)	Percentage of sales written off without appropriate supporting documentation

Chapter summary

- The system of internal controls consists of an effective control environment; the entity's risk assessment process; the entity's process to monitor the system of internal control; the information system and communication; and control activities.
- Control activities in an accounting system address systemic weaknesses and control risks.
- Control activities consist of segregation of duties; physical controls; authorisation and approval of transactions; management controls; supervision controls; organisational controls; arithmetic and accounting controls; and personnel controls. The SPAMSOAP mnemonic may help you remember these.
- The limitations of controls include people making mistakes, where controls may not be operated effectively or where people may deliberately circumvent controls.
- For each control objective within a system, the risks controlled and control activities need to be identified.
- Within any of the systems, segregation of duties – as far as it is possible given the size of the accounting function and the number of its staff – is a vital control.
- Fraud is a crime in which the company suffers a loss because someone either misappropriates assets or misstates information in the financial statements.
- Fraud affects the company in terms of: financial loss; reputational damage; and poor employee morale.
- Fraud controls for the accounting system are categorised as staff, management, physical and computer controls.
- Misappropriation can take the form of: theft of assets; teeming and lading of receipts (receivables ledger) and payments (payables ledger); setting up fictitious suppliers, employees or customers; collusion with customers and suppliers; paying for goods and services not received by the company; and disposal of assets without authority.
- Misstatement of the financial statements arises from: over- or undervaluing inventory; not writing off irrecoverable debts; manipulating accounting estimates to affect profit; fictitious sales; and understating expenses.
- A fraud matrix (or risk matrix) maps potential frauds to the risk to the company and controls over that risk.
- The risk of fraud is graded from low (1) to high (5) on the fraud matrix; more attention is devoted to internal controls over the higher risks.
- Detection controls over fraud comprise spot checks; performance reviews; reconciliation procedures; and control accounts.
- Prevention controls for fraud comprise authorisation; segregation of duties; and review procedures.
- Sales system frauds are typically: stealing cash receipts; overcharging for sales; inflating customer orders; writing off debts; raising credit notes; and teeming and lading.
- Purchases system frauds include ordering goods for own use; paying fictitious suppliers; paying funds into personal bank accounts; and teeming and lading.
- Payroll system frauds may involve: ghost employees; overstating overtime pay; unauthorised increases in pay rates; false expense reimbursements; and retained leavers.

Activity answers

Activity 1: The control environment

Within CCC, **controls are very informal**. Reliance is often based on trust. Formal internal controls would support the accounting system and reduce the possibility of fraud occurring.

Petty cash

No control system is in place. People can help themselves to cash as and when needed; there is no control or reconciliation at the end of each day. Paula is no longer an employee and is still able to help herself to petty cash.

Cash and cheques received in the post are not secured away in a locked drawer or a safe prior to sending to the bank.

Minimal segregation of duties

Stefan opens the post alone and logs the cash and cheques into the day book without any review or verifications in place.

Payroll controls are weak in that Sonja was able to make additional payments to Ron without any authorisation. She also did not verify the payment prior to making it in cash to Ron. There is also the potential that this was not documented, and there is no evidence Ron signed for the additional monies paid to him.

Health and safety regulations are not adhered to – an untrained person using a forklift without having the relevant training. This may be an issue if there was an accident as it is likely that CCC's insurance will be invalid.

The **accounts receivable** system is manual and there has been no regular review by management of the debt recovery process.

The **company cheque book** is not stored securely in a locked drawer or safe and so there is risk that it might be used inappropriately.

Activity 2: Internal controls and ethical standards

Let's start by listing some of the key elements of a system of internal control:

- The control environment
- The entity's risk assessment process
- Processes to monitor the system of internal control
- The information system
- Communication
- Control activities

The following table shows some examples of how each of the five fundamental ethical principles could be met by the use of suitable elements of CCC's system of internal control.

Fundamental ethical principles	Elements of CCC's system of internal control
Integrity	The use of a mission statement, including the aim to act ethically and with integrity, could be considered part of the company's **control environment**.
Objectivity	The use of strategy mapping falls somewhere between **risk assessment** and **monitoring**, and is used by CCC to provide an objective view of the company's future prospects.
Professional competence and due care	All Umteeko fitters are required to have specialist training as a requirement for being a main dealer. This training could be considered one of the company's **control activities**.

Fundamental ethical principles	Elements of CCC's system of internal control
Confidentiality	The company has an **information system** including functions such as payroll, HR and sales, all of which contains sensitive information which the company needs to keep confidential.
Professional behaviour	The financial statements are currently prepared using the services of a local accounting firm, plus there is a separate accounting department, all of which are **control activities** bound by their own standards of expected behaviour.

Tutorial note. Other sensible suggestions would be equally valid: in most instances, organisations make use of **control activities** to achieve their objectives, ethical or otherwise (eg ensuring **integrity** via the use of expenses policies that require invoices and receipts before payment can be authorised, or maintaining standards of **professional behaviour** via a code of conduct).

Activity 3: Potential frauds at CCC

Frauds that could occur within the accounting system could include the following:

(This list is not exhaustive.)

	Potential fraud
Purchases and inventory system	• Theft of assets – computers or other assets could be stolen by any of the staff within CCC due to the easy access to the accounts office. • Theft of inventory – there is no mention of controls such as inventory counts to prevent the theft of inventory from the warehouse. The Excel spreadsheet used to record movements of, or changes to, the level of inventory is also an ineffective control as staff fail to update it. • Overpayment of supplier invoices – there is no control to verify that cheques prepared to pay suppliers equate to the amount owed and invoiced.
Payroll system	• Overstatement of wages – there are no controls in place to approve actual wages paid to staff, so the Sonja, Wages Clerk, could overstate wages by either overpaying on hours worked and/or the hourly rate. • Overstatement of hours worked – the stores supervisor could add more hours to the staff rotas than physically worked by staff. • Monetary theft via the setting up of a ghost employee – there are no controls over the addition of new starters to the payroll system, such as a requirement for documentation that cannot be overridden, segregation of duties, or linking to HR records. This means that a person could set up a fictional employee and keep the wages 'earned' for themselves.

	Potential fraud
Bank and cash system	• Theft of cheques – there are few controls in place to store the cheque book securely, and it is stored in a drawer which is not always locked. • Theft of cash from the office – petty cash is kept in the staff room and there is little control over access to the office. There is no one member of staff responsible for the petty cash tin and the only control is a sheet on which any expenses paid for using petty cash should be logged. However, this control is currently ineffective as it would appear that it is not being used. Staff have also been borrowing money from this tin on occasions. There are frequently discrepancies between the amount that should be in the tin and surprise at finding the tin empty or running low. • Theft of cheques from the mail – no separate controls are in place to record cheques received. • Theft of cash and/or cheques from tills – the tills are not balanced each evening so there is no accountability for any missing cash and/or cheques.
Sales and aged receivables system	• Under-recording of goods sold – there are few controls in place to ensure goods sold are accurately recorded. • Writing off debts – there are no controls to ensure that debts from customers are not written off, or to ensure that they are written off when they should be.

Activity 4: Sales system fraud

(a)

Fraud which could occur at CCC	Why this risk has arisen
Stolen cash receipts through the non-reconciliation of the till records and the cash inside them	The risk is increased by leaving the tills full of cash overnight. Any error or shortfall will not be detected until the next day or when the staff come to reconcile the takings. Having significant amounts of cash on the premises increases the threat of theft or loss.
No credit check undertaken against B. Braithwaite	This is a potential fraud risk as the customer may buy items on credit with no intention of paying (theft of inventory) or the customer may be a fictitious one set up by an unscrupulous member of the sales team who wants to inflate their sales figures for commission payments.
Unallocated cash	Unallocated cash is a fraud risk. There is a risk that sales staff could have diverted funds from a customer and are using more recent cash receipts to try to cover this up, but there will always be a difference if the invoiced amounts do not match.
Writing off debts	All debts require management authorisation to be written off. Currently, debts are written off as and when Stefan believes that they cannot be collected or they have got 'just too old'.

(b) Without management or senior staff performing regular reviews of the aged receivables report, the following issues may occur:

Financial loss

The unallocated cash does not show what debts or final balances need to be settled by customers. By delaying the allocation of cash, it is possible that fraud could occur by 'teeming and lading' (cash receipts being skimmed off and then applying other customer receipts to cover it). By delaying the overall outstanding debt, this type of fraud may only appear if another person performs a reconciliation of the ledger or the customers are contacted directly.

Financial loss due to staff inflating the sales figures and earning more commission.

Financial loss due to inflated sales and risk of overstating VAT liability.

Non-financial

The high level of unallocated cash suggests that customers' invoices may appear to be outstanding when they have in fact been paid. This could adversely affect customer relations if they are chased for debts that they have settled in full.

Equally, with the cheques being dropped and lost when they are received in the post, the risk of paid debts being chased will affect customer relations.

If fraud has occurred, staff morale may drop due to a climate of suspicion.

Activity 5: Purchases system fraud

Ordering goods for own use – there are issues around segregation of duties between ordering, booking goods into inventory and making payments, plus appropriate authorisations. Management should authorise all purchase orders, so that all orders placed can be verified and there are no 'surprises' in value or in finding that staff are using company funds to purchase goods for personal use.

The potential for **fictitious suppliers** – there should be management authorisation of all new suppliers added to the system; reconciliation of payments to invoices; and some segregation of duties for these processes. The new suppliers may all be valid, but management should also be reviewing whether they represent best value in terms of price, quality and credit terms offered.

Invoices incorrectly calculated – CCC may have paid the incorrect amount of £15,000 if this had not been such a significant error and investigated further. Suitable controls would be to match goods received to purchases orders, then matching the invoice to the purchase order when it arrives to check that the supplier has correctly calculated the quantities and prices.

Time wasted – it took Margaret all day to reconcile the manual system to find out what had happened with the incorrectly calculated invoice. If there was a fully integrated system, this would have been highlighted much sooner, and any investigation would have taken significantly less time.

By delaying the payment to the supplier, and not raising the issue earlier, CCC has also risked **affecting the relationship** with this supplier.

Cash flow effect – working capital would have been significantly affected if this £15,000 invoice had been paid, and there is the potential for strained relations with the bank if CCC had asked for an extension to its bank overdraft. Any request to increase the overdraft will result in higher interest charges, as well as possible arrangement fees.

Activity 6: Detecting fraud using financial information

- **Irrecoverable debts** have increased by 175% (whereas revenue has increased by 19%). This suggests that there may be issues regarding the collection of cash or screening of customers (from an earlier activity, we know B. Braithwaite was added with no credit checks). However, from a detection of fraud basis, this could also suggest that cash is being collected from customers and these debts are being written off rather than the cash being applied to them (there was lots of unallocated cash in the most recent aged receivables report). Irrecoverable debts which are written off should also be authorised by a member of management. Management should review a list of the debts (one of the directors last looked at it four months ago) to be written off with explanations as to why this is the case and steps taken to recover any outstanding debt.
- **Sales staff salaries** have increased by 75% which, given the rise of revenue by 19%, is odd. There had been a case of one of the sales staff requesting additional commission and this being paid without being checked. This is a potential area of fraud. Sales commission should be reviewed by the directors prior to being paid. Management should be able to review the sales made by the member of staff (including any credits or refunds given). In order to ensure that credit notes are not being raised after the invoice in order to 'boost' sales, the commission should only be paid after a predetermined period of time (eg quarterly intervals) to allow cut-off testing to be performed.
- **Other costs**: Management should ensure they understand what drives these costs so that they do not simply 'creep up' over time, as many of these should be fixed in nature.
- **Other factors which may be considered**
  - Ensuring that the management accounts are regularly reviewed by the management team
  - Monthly management accounts rather than quarterly would help to highlight any problems most quickly
  - Looking at the actual results against budget to see if the company is 'on track' and the accounts look reasonable

Activity 7: Payroll risks

To: The directors of CCC
Risk assessment of the payroll system based on events in October 20X2
There is a high risk of errors in the payroll system due to: • Unauthorised additional payments to staff taking place • Sales commission not being reviewed and authorised by a member of management (eg the sales manager) prior to payment • New starters being put onto the system without any documentation or confirmations documented regarding their hours, contract and terms and conditions, or whether they actually exist • Large amounts of cash kept on the premises with staff being able to top up wages by taking £1,200 out of petty cash without any safeguards, reviews or authorisation in place • There being no controls over the hours and rates that staff are being paid. There is a risk that these could be amended resulting in staff being paid too much. Risk of regulatory failure due to: • New starters being paid on the system prior to the tax information being received. There is a risk that their deductions will be incorrect, risking penalties from HMRC or complaints from staff affected. • Spoilt payslips being thrown away and not correctly destroyed. This is a confidentiality risk and puts the company at risk of breach of data protection regulations.

- There is no mention of what qualification Sonja currently has or any required continuing professional development. It is possible that new regulations are missed and the company may be fined (eg there is no pension scheme despite this being a legal requirement for all employers in the UK).
- No checks on proof of identity are made, or references required when new staff members join. This could expose the company to risk of theft as well as breaches of money laundering regulations.

Risk of ethical breaches occurring in the workplace due to:

- Bullying and intimidation of payroll staff by members of the sales team (see Ron's treatment of Sonja). All staff should be treated with respect. Aggressive and threatening behaviour should not be tolerated.
- Breach of confidentiality by leaving spoilt payslips with employee information in the bin rather than being destroyed.

Activity 8: Fraud matrix CCC

This fraud matrix suggests improvements to the controls CCC currently has in place. They have to be appropriate to the company; we could not suggest, for instance, full segregation of duties within CCC as there are not enough staff working within the accounting function to make this possible. Also, the assessment of risk is subjective based on our knowledge of the company and the controls currently in place.

Potential fraud	Controls currently in place	Risk to CCC 1 = low, 5 = high	Implications/regulations affected
Theft of assets	Physical access to the accounting function controlled by keypad but with common entry code, and door left propped open.	2	Loss of assets such as computers and possibly key data and information Financial loss
Overstatement of wages – wages clerk Additional monies being paid to staff without the formal support of payroll records	None	4	Overpayment of wages to staff Financial loss
Theft of cash from the office	Petty cash is kept in the staff room and office has keypad access, but door is left propped open. Contains notebook for recording expenses charged to petty cash, but this control is often not followed.	3	Loss of cash
Theft of cheques	Cheque book kept in locked drawer – but control not always followed.	4	Cheques could be used for own purchase/cash Financial loss
Overstatement of hours worked – showroom supervisor	None	3	Overpayment of wages to showroom staff

Potential fraud	Controls currently in place	Risk to CCC 1 = low, 5 = high	Implications/regulations affected
Theft of inventory from warehouse	An Excel spreadsheet showing inventory levels and location of inventory is in place; however, this document is not always updated and inventory reconciliations back to it do not tend to occur.	4	Loss of inventory
Fictitious suppliers could be entered onto the system and payments made	None	4	Financial loss
Overpayment of supplier invoices	None	3	Increased costs Financial loss
Under-recording of goods sold	None	3	Reduced revenue
Writing off customer debts without authorisation	None	3	Financial loss risk due to monies which are recovered being misappropriated whilst the debt is wrongly written off Reputational risk as customer will be unhappy by the chasing of an already paid debt
Theft of cheques from the mail	Cheques received are written into day book by the same person who opens the post. There is no segregation of duties here; it would be better for Stefan to wait until another member of staff is present to witness the opening of post.	2	Lost cheques, reduced revenue Reputational risk as customer will be unhappy by the chasing of an already paid debt
Theft of cash/cheques from the tills	None – tills are not reconciled until the following day.	3	Lost cash/cheques
Theft of wages arising from the payment to a ghost employee	Documentary evidence should be provided before any new starter can be set up on the payroll system; however, there is evidence that this is not always the case.	3	Lost cash/increased costs
Disclosure of staff information without the proper authority	None	3	Potential fine or penalties caused by breach of the data protection Regulations

Potential fraud	Controls currently in place	Risk to CCC 1 = low, 5 = high	Implications/regulations affected
Peter Cookridge buying inventory higher than usual to benefit personally from the supplier who will support his motorcycling	None	4	Cash flow issues Too high an inventory level (affecting working capital) Financial loss Potential breach of the Bribery Act 2010

Test your learning

1 **What type of control activity is each of the following actions? Write your answer in the space provided.**

Action	Type of control activity
Person A matches dispatch notes to invoices; Person B creates invoice to customer	
Control account reconciliation	
Petty cash box kept locked	
Adequate resourcing of accounting function	
Review of budgetary control report	

2 **Complete the following statement:**

Management should regularly ensure that staff perform [▼] of the receivables ledger to ensure accuracy and completeness of the data.

Picklist

- Assessments
- Inspections
- Reconciliations
- Teeming and lading

3 **Complete the following statement:**

Allocating one customer's payment to another customer's account in order to balance the books and detract from a shortfall is called [▼].

Picklist

- Identity fraud
- Inflation
- Reconciliation and review
- Teeming and lading

4 **For each of the following situations where fraud is being discussed, identify the fraud triangle condition that is being described.**

Situation	Fraud triangle condition
'They never check on the older items in the warehouse, so they're the easiest ones to steal.'	▼
'I've worked so hard for this company over the years and yet no-one notices. I'm definitely entitled to take items out of the stationery cupboard for my own personal use.'	▼
'If I don't find the money in the next week, my house will be repossessed by the building society. I have to steal cash from the safe because I have no other way of finding the money I owe.'	▼

Picklist

- Dishonesty
- Opportunity
- Pressure
- Rationalisation

5 **The THREE categories of impact of fraud on a company are:**

	✓
Morale	
Social	
Reputation	
Environmental	
Financial	

6 **Which TWO factors are evaluated to grade the risk of fraud in a fraud matrix?**

	✓
Time	
Responsibility	
Likelihood	
Volatility	
Impact	

7 Which of the following statements is correct?

	✓
During the analysis of the sales system, a fraud matrix graded the potential loss from misappropriation to be rated 5. Management have decided urgent action is required.	
A fraud matrix is a subjective analysis of an organisation's controls, and will ensure that all recommendations identified are actioned immediately.	
A control within the payroll system has been rated as 2 within the fraud matrix. Management have decided that this risk must be rectified immediately.	

3 Accounting systems

Learning outcomes

3.1	**An organisation's accounting system and its effectiveness** Students need to be able to: • Identify the varying financial information requirements of stakeholders (payroll, sales accounting, purchases accounting, general ledger, cash book and costing systems) • Explain how a fully integrated accounting system enables the extraction of information to meet internal and external reporting and monitoring requirements • Identify how an organisation's accounting system can support ethical standards and sustainability practices • Identify weaknesses in accounting systems that impact on cost-effectiveness, reliability and timeliness • Evaluate impact of weaknesses in an accounting system in terms of time, money and reputation
3.2	**The underpinning procedures of an accounting system, assessing the impact on the operation of the organisation** Students need to be able to: • Identify how underpinning procedures in the organisation impact on the operation of the organisation (payroll, authorisation and control of sales, purchases, capital expenditure, overheads, payments and receipts) • Identify how underpinning procedures in the organisation can support ethical standards and sustainability practices • Identify weaknesses in the underpinning procedures and the impact on cost-effectiveness, reliability and timeliness • Evaluate the impact of weaknesses in the underpinning procedures in terms of time, money and reputation

Assessment context

The topics covered in this chapter are most likely to be included in either Task 1 or Task 4 of the Role Scenario Assessment, which test your understanding of ethics and accounting fundamentals and internal control systems respectively.

Qualification context

This chapter builds on content that you will have seen in your previous studies and will complement what you have learned at Level 4 in both Management Accounting and Financial Statements.

Business context

The objective of the accounting system is to provide reliable and timely information for both internal and external stakeholders in a cost-effective manner. Any accounting system will be subject to a number of controls to prevent and detect errors and potential frauds.

By documenting the system, staff can ensure that they are following the correct procedures, and it will assist when new staff join the organisation and act as a reference guide, especially when tasks are performed infrequently.

Underpinning the accounting system is the adherence to the fundamental values of the AAT *Code of Professional Ethics*.

Chapter overview

Accounting systems

- **Accounting systems**
  - Objectives of the accounting system
    - Cost effectiveness
    - Reliability
    - Timeliness
  - The financial information needs of stakeholders
- **Accounting system controls**
  - Documenting the system
    - Flowcharts
    - User manuals
- **Sales system controls**
  - Controls in the sales system
    - Segregation of duties
- **Purchases system controls**
  - Controls in the purchases system
    - Segregation of duties
    - Authorisation
  - Non-current assets
- **Payroll system controls**
- **Security of the accounting system**
  - Limiting access
  - Preventing errors
- **Ethical behaviour within an organisation**
  - Ensuring ethical practice within the accounting system
  - Ethical risks to the system
  - The accounting system, underpinning procedures and sustainability practices

Introduction

In this chapter, we look at some examples of how accounting systems are structured and consider how they provide information to key stakeholders of the company.

We then consider how to assess whether the accounting systems in place (including sales, purchases and payroll) are suitable for the company and whether any improvements could be made to them.

The chapter concludes by considering how the accounting system supports ethical and sustainable business practices.

KEY TERM

Risk: The threat to the company presented by the control objective not being attained.

Management should revisit their controls on a regular basis, checking that the processes designed are actually in place, and that they are being adhered to.

In this chapter, we also look at the importance of monitoring controls, and why this should be completed on a continual basis.

1 Accounting systems

KEY TERM

> **Accounting system:** A system that takes raw data on transactions as its input, processes this data, and then produces many outputs to meet the information needs of stakeholders.

Inputs include:

- Raw data from the accounting transactions
- Data from the users, meaning that all users must have training to ensure accurate usage of the system
- Data from management on subjective areas affected by them – eg journals, provisions and aged receivable adjustments

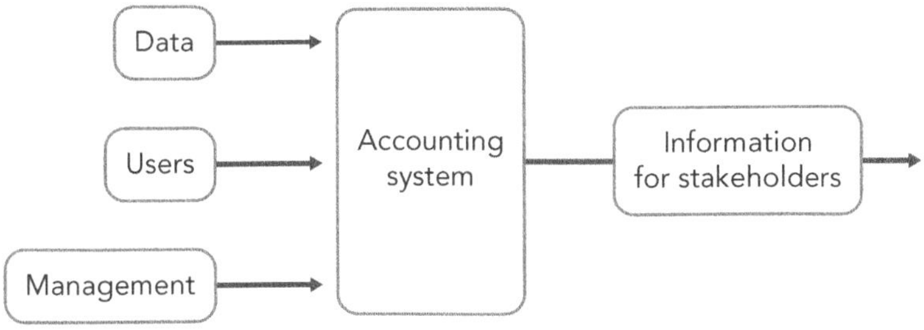

Figure 3.1: Converting data

1.1 Objectives of the accounting system

An accounting system is effective if it meets the following objectives:

1.1.1 Cost effectiveness

KEY TERM

> **Cost effectiveness:** This ensures that something is good value.

Organisations should consider their needs and the complexity of the information they require. The more complex the system, the more expensive it can be to maintain. The cost of training existing staff and new staff on a new or more complex system should be taken into account.

A **large multinational company** will likely have many locations, about which financial information will be required on a timely basis to ensure control. At each of these locations there are likely to be semi-autonomous departments, each having their own specialisms, for instance inventory control, sales orders, purchasing, and preparation of the local management accounts. In large multinational companies of this type, it may be necessary to have a dedicated department to prepare and consolidate the accounts for all the overseas subsidiary companies or branches.

In a **small/medium-sized organisation**, each department may require its own manager(s) (eg purchase manager and sales manager) although, in small organisations, the lines between these managers may be blurred in order to allow holiday and sickness cover.

A **very small organisation** will want to use a more cost-effective, simpler structure, often requiring managers to take on more than one role – eg a single person may be in charge of both the sales and accounting functions. These types of entity will often look to outsource more complex areas of the accountancy function, such as using accountants who will prepare payroll, VAT returns and financial statements on their behalf.

Any changes which are proposed to an accounting system should be carefully considered, weighing up the costs and the benefits of making a change. This is covered in more detail in Chapter 4.

1.1.2 Reliability

KEY TERM

> **Reliability:** This ensures a process or system performs consistently well.

The accounting system must operate effectively, processing all transactions accurately and fully, and must be compliant with applicable laws and regulations. The system should allow access to authorised users only, as and when required, and include data security protocols. A modern system will run regular and automated backups of data. Increasingly companies' data is held offsite 'in the cloud' negating the need for daily, manual backups by users onto discs, USB drives or other hardware that could create cybersecurity risks.

1.1.3 Timeliness

KEY TERM

Timeliness: This means that the system should provide information at the required time.

The accounting function and the underlying system needs to be set up in such a way that the reports are accurate and timely. The system will need to provide financial and management information to stakeholders when they require it. It is vital that the system can produce the information required by its users to enable regulatory compliance (eg quarterly VAT returns) and timely reviews of financial performance.

Staff need sufficient training to ensure that they know what information to produce and when it will be required. They also need to have a good understanding of how to use the software to ensure that it is used in an efficient and accurate manner.

Activity 1: CCC accounting system

Use the information provided about the CCC accounting system in the pre-seen information.

Required

Evaluate the following points:

(a) The cost effectiveness of the CCC accounting system

(b) Its reliability

(c) Do management obtain information in a timely manner?

1.2 The financial information needs of stakeholders

Think back to the start of these materials – you identified a number of stakeholders and considered their information requirements. Let's now think about those information requirements in the context of the **financial information** they will require.

Activity 2: Financial information needs of stakeholders

Previously, we identified the following stakeholders for a typical organisation:

- Owners
- Directors and managers
- Employees
- Customers
- Suppliers
- Lenders
- Government
- Community
- Environment

We also know that accounting systems perform a variety of different tasks:

- Sales accounting
- Purchases accounting
- Payroll
- General ledger
- Cash book
- Costing systems

Required

For each of these stakeholders, describe the financial information that they would typically require from an organisation's accounting system.

2 Accounting system controls

We have already discussed how it is vital that an organisation has a strong and robust system of internal controls.

All systems in the company must be controlled so that they operate efficiently and effectively. Any potential weaknesses in the system need to be mitigated by controls. Just like any other system, any **systemic weaknesses** that arise within the accounting system leave it open to fraud and error.

The accounting system must therefore have built-in controls so that it meets:

- Regulations
- The rules and procedures of the company
- The information requirements of internal and external stakeholders

System controls can include:

- Computer controls (eg passwords or restrictions on staff performing certain operations)
- Manual controls (eg internal audit reviews and supervisory checks)
- Physical controls (eg keypads, locking doors, use of safes and removing cash from tills at night)

2.1 Documenting the system

Systems control starts at the design phase, during which the data flows and processes are mapped. This forms a template for training the users of the system, so that they understand what the system is doing when they are using it. It is vital that these data flows and processes are documented for future reference, in the event that the system breaks down, or needs updating to ensure that it remains fit for purpose.

2.1.1 Flowcharts

All information systems work by receiving inputs, then processing these into outputs. Each stage of the process can be analysed in detail to draw up a simple system flowchart.

KEY TERM

System flowchart: A diagram that shows the flow of the accounting system using boxes and text to show the logic.

Completing a system flowchart enables improvements to the system, and thus to the company's processes, to be identified.

Activity 3: Flowchart of credit control

Using the pre-seen information on CCC, identify the key elements of the accounts receivable process known at this time.

Required

(a) Complete a system flowchart for the accounts receivable function.

(b) Note any gaps in the information which would require further investigation in order to assess the accounting system as it currently stands.

2.1.2 User manuals

Accounting system controls need to be kept under review to ensure they are appropriate and effective, so that the information output from the system is on time and of the correct quality.

KEY TERM

User manual: An accurate analysis of how the accounting system and its controls operate, and how they should be used.

To enable this, the accounting function should maintain an accurate user manual of how the accounting system and its controls operate.

Activity 4: Documentation of controls

CCC is considering developing a full user manual for its accounting system.

Required

(a) What are the advantages of the accounting system having a full user manual for all activities that take place within it?

(b) What might the disadvantages of such an approach be for an organisation like CCC?

3 Sales system controls

The various parts of the accounting system require different internal controls. Here, we look at the types of **controls** that are found in sales systems, and the **risks** or **weaknesses** that they are designed to mitigate.

Cash sales are particularly risky, as when a company makes a cash sale no credit is granted. As the customer chooses and pays for goods on the spot, no formal order is raised, resulting in inventory being issued without a sales order form. The risks this poses are discussed later.

In this section, we focus on the correct actions which need to take place to ensure controls are in place. These are the **control objectives** of the credit sales system, and the risks inherent within.

3.1 Controls in the sales system

3.1.1 Segregation of duties

Dividing tasks among several staff members in the sales system, especially in relation to handling cheques and cash receipts, is a key control. By ensuring that one member of staff completes a task, and another reviews the process, it is easier to prevent and detect the following frauds and errors:

(a) **Ghost customers** – creating a false customer who orders goods but does not pay (in effect stealing the company's inventory). This is possible if the same person is in charge of orders and credit control/accounts receivable (receivables ledgers). This risk is mitigated by segregation of duties (eg new customers are approved by management, then a different employee enters them onto the system following an external credit check).

(b) **Stolen cash receipts** – cash received is not recorded in the ledgers; it is stolen by employees. Alternatively, an employee could intercept cheques when they arrive and steal them before they are recorded. Segregation of duties is operated here by having the person opening the post supervised during the process.

(c) **Overcharging on sales** – goods sold are overcharged, with employees keeping the additional amount received from customers.

(d) **Inflating customer orders** – additional goods are added to a customer's order but not invoiced to them. Instead, the excess inventory is retained by the employee for their own use, or to sell on privately.

(e) **Writing off debts** – writing off amounts owed when in fact the debt was paid in full. The employee then keeps the written-off amount.

(f) **Raising credit notes** – that are not sent to the customer, who therefore pays in full. When payment is received in full, the employee keeps the cash matching the false credit amount.

(g) **Teeming and lading** – allocating one customer's payment to another in order to balance the books and detract from a shortfall.

KEY TERM

Authorisation of transactions: This is a key control activity, indicating to accounting staff that the transaction in question is valid.

Activity 5: Sales controls (1) – customers and orders

The following describes the procedures which CCC currently uses for accepting new customers, taking sales orders and the delivery process.

While some customers pay cash for their goods, over 60% take credit terms. Customers are granted 28 days to pay their invoice in full, interest free. CCC uses a credit reference agency for orders over £200 to ensure that potential new credit customers have no history of poor payments. Once the agency has done this check, the customer is automatically granted an unlimited line of credit. The sales staff are in charge of calling the credit agency at the time of sale but, as Stefan had recently identified, this does not always happen if junior staff are on duty, or it is a busy day of sales.

All new credit accounts are set up on the first day of the calendar month. All sales orders are received by the showroom store staff for processing, and after completion are passed to the accounting function the next morning, so that Stefan can prepare and record the invoices. Stefan has designed a form in Microsoft Word that he uses as a template for invoicing. All invoices are logged onto an Excel spreadsheet which can be accessed by the accounting team.

The operations manager asks Stefan for a copy of the Excel spreadsheet so he can plan the deliveries for the next week. Once this schedule has been drawn up, the inventory is identified and marked up for delivery. A dispatch note is drawn up and this is handed to the customer. The dispatch note is a manual form which details the customer's address and the invoice reference.

CCC contacts the customers a few days beforehand to agree a delivery time. If the flooring is to be fitted, then the name of the fitter will be supplied. When the flooring has been delivered and fitted, the fitter hands the delivery note to the customer who retains it. The customer does not pay the fitter.

Required

(1) Identify the controls in place at CCC for the sales system; and

(2) Explain the control activities from the control objectives supplied, noting any risks/weaknesses and making any recommendations for improvement.

Control objective	Control activity	Risk/weakness and recommendations
Completeness of recording sales		
Invoices recorded in the correct time period		
Only creditworthy customers are offered credit terms		
Record goods dispatched in the inventory system		

Activity 6: Sales controls (2) – Credit control

The following information has been obtained regarding the cash collection procedures at CCC.

> **CCC credit control policies**
>
> The company policy regarding non-payment is as follows:
>
> - Once payment is seven days overdue, Stefan will telephone the customer.
> - If payment is not received within 14 days of the telephone call, Stefan will write to the customer requesting payment and for the account to be brought into order.
> - If payment is still not received within the next 14 days, the customer's details are passed on to a debt collection agency which works on behalf of the company. The debt collection agency charges £80 per case, plus 30% of any monies collected.
>
> Though this is the policy, the directors of CCC rarely bother following it through.
>
> As the invoices are manually input onto Word templates, set up by Stefan, he must create an Excel spreadsheet each month to look at what money is owed. He usually rolls forward the spreadsheet from the previous month, but as he is very busy and management do not prompt him, he sometimes misses a month.
>
> Stefan opens the mail every morning and sorts through it. Any cheques received from customers are entered manually into a day book to record the receipt. The day book is then used to update the ledger accounts, and the cheques are placed in the office safe until a banking day.
>
> At the end of every day, all cash and cheques are supposed to be removed from the tills, leaving a float of £100 cash in each till for the start of the next day. The principle is that the till should be balanced to ensure that the cash content is correct.
>
> However, during the week this does not happen as the sales staff feel that they should not be asked to do an extra job after closing. The first salesperson in the next day counts the till contents and takes it upstairs to the accounting office for Stefan to bank it.
>
> As a result, it is common practice that all cash (except for the till floats) and cheques are removed and bagged as takings from individual tills before being stored in the safe in the accounting function office.
>
> **Banking**
>
> Banking is carried out on Monday and Thursday, and this is normally Stefan's job, which he does during his lunch break.
>
> Recently, available cash from the office safe has been used to pay wages in order to reduce the amount of money drawn from the bank via cheques.

Required

(1) Identify the controls in place at CCC for credit control and cash collection; and

(2) Explain the control objectives and activities, noting any risks/weaknesses and making any recommendations for improvement.

Control objective	Control activity	Risk/weakness and Recommendations
Record all invoiced sales in the accounting records (receivables ledger and general ledger).		

Control objective	Control activity	Risk/weakness and Recommendations
Record invoiced sales in the correct receivables ledger accounts.		
Identify debts for which payment might be doubtful.		
Record all money received.		
Bank all money received.		
Safeguard money received until it is banked.		

4 Purchases system controls

The purchases system – from placing an order to paying the supplier's invoice – is a part of the accounting system which it is particularly important to have controls over because:

(a) The purchases system involves **receiving inventory** and **paying cash** – arguably the two types of asset which are most open to fraud and theft.

(b) Purchases may be of **very high value** if the company is incurring capital expenditure.

(c) Information from the purchases system becomes part of the data which supports the costing system. Errors and fraud in purchasing will lead to **inaccurate information** being used for planning, decision making and performance measurement.

(d) The purchase of inventory will affect any manufacturing or retail process. If the information is not accurate, there is a risk of **delays** to the manufacturing process or delays in fulfilling orders from customers.

4.1 Controls in the purchases system

4.1.1 Segregation of duties

Once again, segregation of duties is vital. The chief concern is that a person could order and pay for personal goods through the company, so ordering and payment should be separated.

The risk of fraud will also be reduced if the person who authorises invoices for payments is independent of the person clearing the payment itself.

4.1.2 Authorisation

All purchases should be authorised; however, it would be impractical to have one person authorise every item of expenditure, especially if it required often and in large quantities. To mitigate for this, accounting systems often have set levels of approval for regular purchases, with monitoring controls by management to review weekly or monthly expenditure reports. Often, there will be maximum amount, above which there is a requirement for management approval, such as £10,000 for a line manager and £50,000 for a director.

Activity 7: Purchases system controls

The following is a summary of the CCC purchases control system:

All inventory is purchased on credit terms from a wide range of suppliers. This is one of Peter Cookridge's roles, and he enjoys researching new inventory lines. He also likes meeting the sales staff from suppliers. He has a favourite group of suppliers he tends to use, mainly because they sponsor his motorbike racing efforts. There is no formal list of suppliers.

Margaret Peterson has worked on Excel previously, but this was over ten years ago. While she is competent at inputting data, she sometimes struggles with anything beyond this.

Inventory is ordered by Margaret, who receives the request from the warehouse staff, often verbally, especially if the customer needs the goods urgently. The larger suppliers do provide next-day delivery, which is very useful for CCC.

When the inventory arrives in the warehouse, it is signed for by whomever is available in the warehouse. They should check for any damage, but time is usually at a premium, and so most of the junior staff will just accept a delivery and move it to a space in the store. The goods received note (GRN) is put in the in-tray and is taken up to the accounts department when the tray gets full, which is usually once a week.

Margaret will input the invoices she receives (Stefan opens the post and will bring any invoices into the office that same morning) onto the Excel spreadsheet, detailing the following:

- Supplier name
- Description of the item purchased (including dimensions)
- Cost price

If Margaret has a GRN which matches an invoice, she will clip them together and file them away. She uses her Excel spreadsheet as the basis for running the end of month supplier pay run.

Suppliers are paid at the end of the month in which their invoice is received, as long as funds are available. However, some suppliers now request payment within 30 days of the date of invoice, and this is beginning to cause John Cookridge some concern.

CCC holds a large inventory, with many rolls (often older or discontinued ranges) of carpet in the warehouse for sale on a cash basis.

All suppliers are paid by cheque. These are completed by Margaret, and then signed by either John or Peter as they are now the only authorised signatories. The cheque book is stored in a drawer in Margaret's desk in the accounting function office. Occasionally, when the brothers are away from the office for a few days they pre-sign some cheques so that Margaret can make any emergency payments in their absence.

Required

(1) Note FOUR key weaknesses in the CCC purchase and inventory system; and

(2) Highlight the risk and propose a suitable control to be implemented by management.

Weakness	Control proposed	Risk controlled

4.2 Non-current assets

Generally, non-current assets purchases are less frequent purchases for an organisation, but the same rules apply in that the expenditure should be **authorised**.

An organisation will have established rules regarding the purchase of non-current assets, which may look something like this:

Identify the need for the asset → Agree a budget → Obtain quotations from suppliers → Purchase asset → Authorise payment

Figure 3.2: Process for purchasing non-current assets

Generally, the budget for a new non-current asset will be approved by a member of the management team, but sometimes, in larger organisations there may be a Budget Committee who will make large, financial decisions. In both cases, a business case together with initial expenditure, estimated payback and useful life will be part of the report submitted for approval.

Increasingly, organisations will want to see what the tax implications would be on such large purchases (eg what are the capital allowances) are there any grants available, maybe the land to be developed is in an area which attracts government funding.

The organisation is likely to have an approved list of suppliers, and several quotations will be obtained to ensure the most suitable price, terms and conditions of purchase.

The payment to be authorised will be agreed against the budgeted figure, and any discrepancies investigated.

5 Payroll system controls

Payroll is a high-risk area, with the segregation of duties and a review of the amounts to be paid mandatory to ensure a robust control environment. Risks are increased if the payroll is run manually and cash is the main basis for payment to staff.

Activity 8: CCC – payroll controls

The following is some information regarding the payroll system at CCC.

Until six months ago, the payroll was completed by the company's accountants, Bright & Co. Sonja now runs the payroll on a weekly and monthly basis.

The warehouse, delivery and fitting staff are paid weekly in cash. Pay packets are available from the showroom and marketing manager, Jim Andrews, from 10:00 am on a Friday morning.

The rest of the staff are paid monthly, by BACS, on the last working day of each month.

Sales staff earn a commission of 2% on the first £7,500 of sales per month, and 5% on any sales over that figure. John Cookridge is responsible for preparing staff rotas to ensure that there is adequate staff coverage for all opening hours. Most of the sales staff are willing to work overtime, so this does not usually create any problems.

Fitters are assigned to their respective duties on a weekly basis and are usually notified on a Monday morning when they arrive at work.

Once the week has finished, the completed rotas are given to Sonja, who uses them to calculate the amount of hours that the individual employees have worked.

Sonja prepares the payslips from this information on a Wednesday, calculating manually any overtime payments due and any Sunday working. From this, she calculates how much cash needs to be drawn from the bank and uses the company cheque book (which is kept locked in Margaret's desk) to prepare a cheque ready for signing.

On a Thursday, she prepares the pay packets, which are then stored in the office safe for Jim to collect and hand out to the staff the following day – although any member of sales staff who is not busy will actually do this. Any pay packets not given out are returned to the office safe by Sonja and remain there until collected by the relevant member of staff.

Salaried staff are paid monthly on the last working day of the month, and this is done using BACS. The BACS information is prepared by Sonja, signed by either of the directors, and needs to be with the bank by the 25th of each month. The directors will agree the salaried staff payments to Sonja's calculation schedule. Sonja can input the details onto the bank system for the payments and can authorise the payments up to a value of £10,000 per BACS run. This is adequate to cover the salaried staff, except if the commissions are high or at Christmas. Then, the BACS run must be further authorised on the banking software by one of the authorised signatories. No further checks are made by the directors.

Envelopes with payslips are handed to each member of the salaried staff by Sonja on the day they are paid. If a staff member is not available, the envelope is placed in their desk drawer.

There is no requirement, or system in place, for either store or office employees to sign in or out when they start or finish work.

Required

(1) **Document the payroll controls currently in place at CCC; and**

(2) **Consider where any control weaknesses lie, and what control activities should be introduced to mitigate risks to the company.**

Payroll control in place	Control weakness	Suggested control to be introduced

Assessment focus point

The activities in this chapter are to enable you to practise identifying the key risks, weaknesses and controls in place in different systems. In the assessment, you may be asked specific questions regarding controls over trade receivables (consider the sales cycle), inventory and work in progress (think about purchases controls). Consider also the differences between service, manufacturing and retail industries.

6 Security of the accounting system

The accounting system must be secure so that it can perform its function. This can be done in a number of ways, for instance preventing initial access to the system with a physical barrier (locks on the doors) or using passwords to prevent unauthorised access to the software.

KEY TERM

Physical controls: Ensure assets such as inventory and cash are safe.

Information processing controls: Controls relating to the transactions and standing data in the computerised accounting system.

Integrity controls: To verify and validate input data, the processing of data and the production of reports.

6.1 Limiting access

KEY TERM

Security controls: Controls in the accounting system that cover integrity controls, system controls and physical access controls.

All users of a computerised accounting system should have a password that only gives them access to the parts of the system they are authorised to use. This ensures staff cannot complete operations that are not related to their role – eg access to payroll systems will be strictly limited to HR staff.

Management should guard against malicious or fraudulent access using a variety of **security controls**, such as physical barriers (locks on doors and cabinets), deterrents (alarm system or security), IT controls (passwords, firewalls and ensuring adequate disaster recovery processes are in place, eg backups of data) and monitoring of controls (management reviews, authorisation requirements, etc).

Such controls in the accounting system include implementing **integrity controls**.

There should be **information processing controls** over standing data to ensure only authorised changes are made; for example, new suppliers can only be entered onto a system by an authorised person, or payroll data only accessible by payroll staff.

Ensuring strict segregation of duties by reducing the number of people involved in different parts of each process and minimising the opportunity for fraud and error will help to ensure the integrity of standing data and ensuring only authorised transactions are made.

KEY TERM

Integrity of data: Ensures that data is complete, secure and accurate.

6.2 Preventing errors

The accounting system should have robust integrity controls to verify and validate input data, the processing of data and the production of reports.

These should include **input controls** on completeness of data input to the system (eg batch processing, total checks, not allowing journals to be posted which do not balance). There can also be programme controls ensuring the accuracy of data input to the system, such as an automatic check on the calculation of VAT. Some controls, such as integrity controls, confirm the consistency and validity of the data being entered, such as the correct format of figures (eg allowing invoice numbers in the correct format, AA12345) and the accurate calculation of VAT. They are rules in the system which allow only certain types of data to be inserted.

KEY TERM

> **Processing controls:** May be used to warn the user if they try to log out before processing is finished or close a document prior to saving. Data is also checked for arithmetical accuracy.

Processing controls verify the **data validation** and **editing procedures**. They can also ensure that forms are not closed without being saved or can only be altered by one user at a time. They also used for ensuring **arithmetical accuracy** or **completeness** of data. One example of this is 'batch invoice processing' whereby the total value of the invoices is independently calculated and then the total of the invoices entered onto the system is verified against this total.

Activity 9: Security and IT at CCC

Below is an extract from the CCC IT policy currently in place.

> All computers can only be accessed by staff who have been authorised by management to use CCC's computers. All computers must be password protected.
>
> Computers must only be loaded with licensed software owned by the company. No changes to software are permitted without the consent of CCC's directors. No member of staff is allowed to load any software onto computers without prior permission from management.
>
> No unauthorised devices are to be used for saving, uploading or downloading work (eg discs, memory sticks, external hard drives or other devices) other than those purchased and approved by the company.
>
> Computers should only be used for company business and must not be used to access any social networking sites.

Required

Using the information available in the pre-seen information on CCC, comment on the following:

(a) What rules should be put in place regarding the use of and control of passwords at CCC?

(b) Why are these important?

(c) Note any other issues regarding the current security of the accounting system and IT practice at CCC.

7 Ethical behaviour within an organisation

In your previous studies, you would have considered the impact of the organisation's size, culture and type on its accounting function. Here, we consider how **ethical principles** should guide the practices and controls within an accounting system.

Management should ensure that these principles are embedded within the organisation's accounting system.

> **Assessment focus point**
>
> Ensure you have a thorough understanding of the five fundamental principles of professional ethics. If you need to revisit these areas, review your Level 3 course materials for more details.

7.1 Ensuring ethical practice within the accounting system

Management and directors need to ensure that ethical practice is maintained within their organisation. Often, there will be an organisational **policy** or **mission statement** or a **code of conduct** that employees are expected to follow.

Activity 10: Ensuring ethical behaviour at work

CCC has recently revised its website, adding information regarding its mission statement (see Chapter 1). Stefan, the accounts receivable clerk, has suggested that the five ethical principles as set out by the AAT *Code of Professional Ethics* (the *Code*) be added to the website. The directors have agreed and intend to show how CCC's accounting function (and all other staff) achieves these principles in order to demonstrate what an ethical organisation it is in practice.

Required

Using the table below, identify how CCC can ensure its accounting function (and all other staff) uphold the ethical standards demanded by the *Code*.

Fundamental ethical principle	Explain how CCC may demonstrate these principles in practice
Integrity	
Objectivity	
Professional competence and due care	

Fundamental ethical principle	Explain how CCC may demonstrate these principles in practice
Confidentiality	
Professional behaviour	

7.2 Ethical risks to the system

The **control environment** plays an important role in establishing and maintaining the ethical culture within an organisation. **Risks** to ethical behaviour may come in a variety of forms:

- **Criminal behaviour** (bribery, money laundering, theft)
- **Non-compliance** with organisational policy or regulations (data protection, the *Code*)
- **Bullying** or **intimidating** behaviour
- **Poor decision making** (short-term decision making, reputational risks, environmental hazards)

Let us consider some ethical issues concerning CCC's accounting function in line with these fundamental principles.

Activity 11: Ethical conflicts at CCC

Consider the following scenarios:

(1) Stefan is asked to produce an aged receivables listing for John Cookridge as at 30 April 20X3. However, he does not have up to date figures because cash received has not yet been allocated to customers, and Stefan knows that the aged receivables report will look worse than the underlying situation. Sonja suggests that to get the report done in time he should use averages for the missing figures.

(2) Margaret has opened a letter from an estate agent requesting financial information about one of CCC's customers, who is applying to rent a property. The information is needed as soon as possible, by email, in order to secure approval for the rental agreement.

(3) A friend tells Stefan on a night out that she expects to inherit money from a recently deceased uncle. She asks him how she will be affected by inheritance tax, capital gains tax and other matters.

(4) A supplier is so pleased with how promptly Stefan paid her that she offers him a free weekend break in a luxury hotel, just as a 'thank you'.

Required

Identify the ethical issues at risk in the scenarios and recommend a course of action to be taken by Stefan or Margaret in each case.

7.3 The accounting system, underpinning procedures and sustainability practices

In addition to considering how an organisation's accounting system and underpinning procedures support **ethical standards**, you also need to be able to identify how these elements support **sustainability practices**.

We have already discussed ethical and sustainability issues in the context of **external reporting**. How do these elements support the achievement of an organisation's **sustainability practices**? Let's consider some definitions to help with your understanding.

KEY TERM

> **Sustainability practices:** Policies, procedures and actions designed to support the achievement of an organisation's sustainability objectives.
>
> **Sustainability objectives:** Goals or targets linked to desirable sustainability outcomes, activities and behaviour.

What do desirable **sustainability outcomes, activities and behaviours** look like? What kind of **policies** and **procedures** might an organisation deploy to achieve them? In many respects, this will depend on what an organisation does but, in general, this could include the following:

- Responsible consumption of resources (eg electricity, water, and other raw materials)
- Reduction of wastage
- Increased use of recycling and recycled materials in production
- Efficient forms of activity (including transportation) that reduce fuel usage and emissions
- Fair treatment of people in business activities

There may be **additional sustainability practices** that lead to more desirable sustainability-related outcomes:

- **Innovation** that leads to more sustainable products and services – eg the invention of flooring that lasts longer than existing products, reducing the amount of flooring that requires replacement
- **Government action** designed to promote or discourage certain behaviour in both organisations and individuals – eg incentive schemes to promote the use of more sustainable materials in the manufacture of flooring products

Activity 12: How systems and procedures support sustainability practices

How can an organisation's accounting system and underpinning processes support the achievement of its sustainability objectives?

Chapter summary

- The accounting system processes raw data on transactions into outputs to meet the information needs of stakeholders.
- An effective accounting system operates effectively, reports accurately, and complies with applicable laws and regulations.
- Controls in an accounting system allow it to effectively and accurately meet internal and external regulations, and the information needs of stakeholders.
- Internal controls in the accounting system aim to:
  - Protect it from systemic weaknesses;
  - Avoid fraudulent activities and human error;
  - Ensure compliance with applicable laws and regulations; and
  - Ensure the company is working to meet its objectives.
- Control activities in an accounting system address systemic weaknesses and control risks.
- A user manual documents the accounting system and enables its effectiveness to be kept under review.
- Flowcharting the accounting system and internal controls enables a systems analyst to see whether controls have been designed effectively.
- In the credit sales system, control objectives (etc) are identified for:
  - Taking orders and extending credit;
  - Dispatching and invoicing goods;
  - Recording and accounting for sales and returns; and
  - Receiving payment.
- In the purchases system, control objectives etc are identified for ordering, receipt of goods and services, accounting, and payments.
- In the payroll system, control objectives etc are identified for: setting wages and salaries; recording; payments; and deductions.
- Threats to the accounting system's security include human error, data loss, malicious damage, and fraud.
- Security controls include controls over the integrity of data and processing, the system itself, and physical access to the system.
- Information processing controls affect transactions and consist of input controls, accuracy controls, authorisation checks, processing controls and controls over standing data.
- General IT controls protect the general computer environment.
- Using and updating strong passwords are key security controls.
- The fundamental principles of professional ethics are:
  - Integrity
  - Objectivity
  - Professional competence and due care
  - Confidentiality
  - Professional behaviour
- The accounting system needs to be operated in an ethical manner, following the five fundamental principles, in order to meet its objectives.
- Organisations can also use their accounting system and underpinning processes to help them pursue sustainability practices.

Activity answers

Activity 1: CCC accounting system

(a) The current IT system is Microsoft Office based and CCC does not use a bespoke or 'off the shelf' accounting system such as Sage or a cloud accounting system such as Xero. There are therefore no annual or monthly fees, making this a very cheap system to maintain.

However, most of the activities that the staff are required to do, such as raising invoices and preparing summary reports, take longer to complete because they use a Word template and this requires manual calculations.

Due to the manual nature of most of the transactions completed by staff, this can make the accounting system overly time-consuming to update and use, as well as more open to human error.

(b) Information is produced by the team when requested by management, apart from the quarterly reports set as standard (summary of financial revenue and expenses and a budgetary control report).

Although management have not yet noticed any issues regarding reliability of the IT system, the computers used by the staff are all 'stand-alone' and do not network. Therefore, the computers do not 'talk' to each other, and information may be missed or even duplicated. Currently, only one member of staff actively backs up their data. There is a high risk that data may be lost if the computers crash. There is a risk that the information produced may be inconsistent with reporting requirements – eg accuracy of the VAT and PAYE reporting due to the manual calculations involved.

(c) Given the manual element of the system, it takes longer and is more labour intensive to prepare internal reports, such as management accounts. The management accounts are only prepared quarterly for this reason, and it can take up to 20 days for them to be completed. Whilst this seems slow, it may be entirely acceptable to the directors of CCC.

Overall: Although the current IT system costs little to maintain, it is not cost effective in terms of usage due to the manual nature of the processes undertaken by staff. This causes information output delays, and there is also a risk of data loss.

Activity 2: Financial information needs of stakeholders

The following is an illustration of the various stakeholders and how each of them might use the various elements of the accounting system. You can see that not all of them will apply (eg the environment has no interest in, or use for, financial information).

	Sales accounting	Purchases accounting	Payroll	General ledger	Cash book	Costing systems
Owners	Shareholders of an organisation would have little need for financial information at such a specific level – headline information (eg profits, dividends and prospects) would be of greater use. However, partners or proprietors (ie owner/managers) would be far more interested in all of this information to understand their business – especially issues such as cash availability and overall general ledger reporting.					
Directors/ managers	Senior leadership staff may not deal with these parts of the accounting system directly, but would still be interested in the output of each one – eg to compare sales volumes and values with budgets, to analyse payroll costs or to identify variances in costing systems. In all of these, the information would be used to assist them in their leadership of the organisation.					
Employees	The extent of employees' interest in financial information would usually depend on their role (eg if working within the finance department, these would be of critical importance to them). However, employees with no financial involvement may only be interested in the payroll information they receive – eg payslips, P60s, and other tax or employment-related documentation.					
Customers	Invoices Receipts	N/A				

<table>
<tr><th></th><th>Sales accounting</th><th>Purchases accounting</th><th>Payroll</th><th>General ledger</th><th>Cash book</th><th>Costing systems</th></tr>
<tr><th>Suppliers</th><td>N/A</td><td>Orders
Payment</td><td colspan="4">N/A</td></tr>
<tr><th>Lenders</th><td colspan="6">This would depend on the nature of the financing in place (eg long-term debt or short-term overdraft) but, in general, lenders would have no interest in any of these elements of the accounting system because their main focus is on the payment of interest and the repayment of capital (of greater interest would be published external financial statements and other data such as share prices which would alert them to any risk of default).</td></tr>
<tr><th>Government</th><td colspan="2">N/A</td><td>Tax paid
Deductions
Benefits
Pensions</td><td colspan="3">N/A</td></tr>
<tr><th>Community</th><td colspan="6">There may be instances where members of the local community have some form of financial involvement with an entity (eg fundraising or donations) where they interact in financial terms. Otherwise, the main focus for communities is the social impact that an organisation has, so much of this financial information is irrelevant.</td></tr>
<tr><th>Environment</th><td colspan="6">N/A</td></tr>
</table>

Activity 3: Flowchart of credit control

(a) System flowchart:

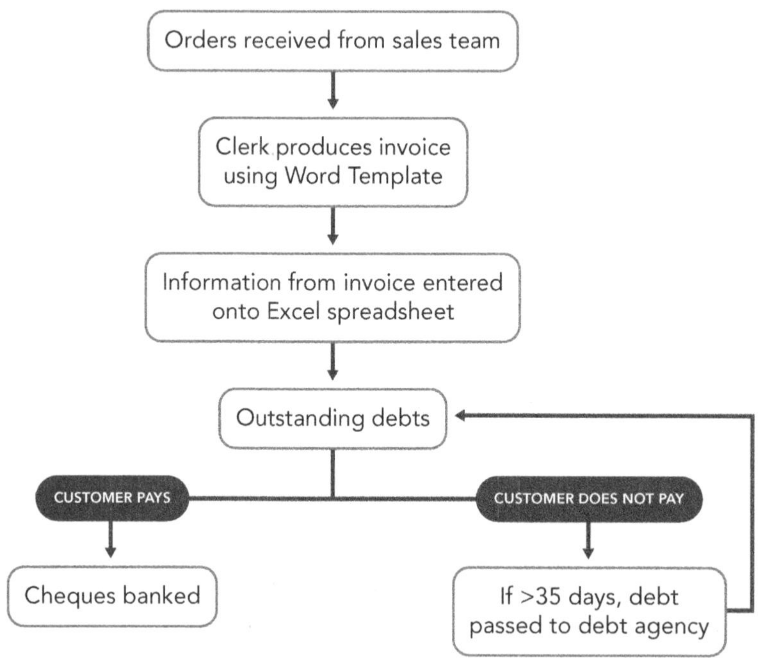

(b) Information which needs to be investigated further to ensure the flowchart is complete and to fully assess the accounting system for credit control:

- How are the debts chased by the team; are the customers phoned or letters written? Who is responsible for this role?
- Does management ever review the aged receivables report to decide whether any debts need to be classified as irrecoverable?
- What happens if the debt collection agency is unsuccessful?
- Can customers pay directly via BACS? How are these receipts identified and allocated to customers' accounts?

Activity 4: Documentation of controls

(a) Advantages of a user manual for CCC's accounting system:

- Quick and efficient training of new staff
- Better visibility of the controls in place
- Consistent approach to completing activities
- Easier to rotate staff between roles and responsibilities
- Easier to evaluate staff against standard procedures
- Improved supervisory and management control

(b) Disadvantages of a user manual:

- There is increased risk of 'outsiders' being able to operate the system, especially as the door to the accounting function is usually left open and the office unsecured.
- Procedures may stifle innovation and improvements to processes.
- User manuals take time to complete, and the accounting function at CCC is very short on resources currently. This may take up too much time to the detriment of the day-to-day business.
- The manuals may become out of date quickly and a small company like CCC may not have time to regularly review and update the manuals.
- The manuals need to be tested to ensure they accurately reflect the systems in place.
- Staff often do not conform to manuals, negating the benefits of having them.

Activity 5: Sales controls (1) – customers and orders

Control objective	Control activity	Risk/weakness and recommendations
Completeness of recording sales	Sales orders are manually entered onto the system.	There is no pre-ordered invoice numbering, which allows for orders to be missed (customers taking goods without being invoiced). Manual system is open to error as the invoices are manually calculated on a Word template. Customer may be incorrectly invoiced, which could lead to loss of revenue or reputation if a customer is charged in error. Recommendation: To buy an integrated accounting system with orders matching to invoices which are system calculated with pre-numbered invoices to ensure completeness.

Control objective	Control activity	Risk/weakness and recommendations
Invoices recorded in the correct time period	Implement cut-off procedures (eg at each month-end review) to ensure outstanding orders are recorded in the correct month.	Invoices for new customers are not set up until the next month, so invoices are not recorded in the correct period. New customers should be set up prior to sales being authorised.
Only creditworthy customers are offered credit terms	Credit checks on all orders over £200 should be completed at the point of sale.	There is a risk that CCC may incur financial losses due to not all customers being credit checked. Staff should be trained on how the checks are completed. Manager authorisation of initial credit sales to new customers should be established to ensure that all sales with credit terms have been adequately checked. The unlimited credit line should be replaced with hard limits that can only be increased with the authority of the directors once a track record of reliable payment has been established.
Record goods dispatched in the inventory system	Inventory should be marked up for delivery and a dispatch note manually raised.	Dispatch of goods should be authorised by appropriate personnel and agreed back to order documents. Dispatched goods should be inspected for quality and quantity. Dispatch notes should be sequentially numbered and the sequence should be checked regularly. Inventory records should be updated from goods sent out records. Unfulfilled orders should be regularly reviewed.

Activity 6: Sales controls (2) – Credit control

Control objective	Control activity	Risk/weakness and Recommendations
Record all invoiced sales in the accounting records (receivables ledger and general ledger).	Sales invoice sequence should be recorded and spoilt invoices recorded and destroyed.	Sales not recorded and wrongly omitted from financial statements Payment not chased as the sale was never recorded Perform regular reconciliations between sales invoices and receivables ledgers
Record invoiced sales in the correct receivables ledger accounts.	Receivables statements should be prepared and checked regularly. This is especially important with CCC as it has a manual system where invoices are input onto a spreadsheet, so the margin for error is greater. Receivables statements should be safeguarded so they cannot be amended before they are sent out (password protected). Accounts receivable control account should be reconciled regularly to the receivables ledger.	Loss of custom by chasing the wrong customer for the debt Not receiving the money from the correct customer If the invoice is not entered onto the sales Excel spreadsheet, the debt may not get chased at all. This is one of the reasons CCC should consider a more integrated system.
Identify debts for which payment might be doubtful.	Overdue accounts should be reviewed and followed up. There should be a regular review of the aged receivables report by staff and by management. Write-off of irrecoverable debts should be authorised by appropriate personnel.	Failure to take action until it is too late to recover the debt Irrecoverable debts misstated as assets in the financial statements Currently, CCC has no regular review process for the aged receivables and no formalised method of reviewing the write-off of irrecoverable debts. Risk that valid and recoverable debts may be incorrectly written off

Control objective	Control activity	Risk/weakness and Recommendations
Record all money received.	Supervise opening the post to avoid interception. There should be appropriate arrangements made when cashiers are on holiday. Receipts books should be serially numbered and kept locked up. Sales receipts should be matched with invoices. Customer remittance advices should be retained.	Money stolen or lost Custom lost through chasing payments already made by the customer Financial statements misstated Risk that only one person opening the post and also recording any payments received may contribute to fraud or loss of cash or cheques (intentional or otherwise) Customers should be encouraged to pay via online banking or using cards in the shop.
Bank all money received.	Till rolls should be reconciled to cash collections which should then be agreed to cash banked. Cash and cheques should be banked daily. All receipts should be banked together. Where card payments are taken in the shop, the card reader end-of-day report should reconcile to the card payments received in the till.	Money could be stolen or lost as banking is currently only completed twice a week. Custom lost through chasing payments already made by the customer Financial statements misstated. Company cannot earn interest on money if it is not banked, or pays additional overdraft interest.

Control objective	Control activity	Risk/weakness and Recommendations
Safeguard money received until it is banked.	There should be restrictions on who is allowed to accept cash (cashiers or salespeople). Cash received should be evidenced (till rolls, receipts). Cash registers should be regularly emptied. Cash shortages should be investigated. Opening of new bank accounts should be restricted to certain personnel and authorised by senior management. Cash floats held should be limited. Restrictions should be in place when making payments from cash received. Restrictions should be in place for access to cash on the premises. Cash floats should be checked by an independent person, sometimes on a surprise basis. Cash should be locked up outside normal business hours.	Money may be stolen in the interim period. Differences between the sales recorded in the tills and the cash actually received may go unnoticed and errors occur in the financial records. Banking should be more regular, and the company should consider only accepting payment via card to avoid cash-based risks altogether.

Activity 7: Purchases system controls

Any four from the following examples:

Weakness	Control proposed	Risk controlled
Goods and services can be ordered for any purpose – personal or the company's benefit.	Necessity for orders should be evidenced before orders are authorised. Only prepare orders when purchase requisitions are received from relevant departments. Pre-number and safeguard blank order forms. Orders not yet received should be reviewed.	Company pays for unnecessary or personal goods.
Any suppliers can be used – no approved list.	Have a central policy for choosing suppliers. Monitor supplier terms and take advantage of discounts offered.	Unauthorised suppliers may not supply quality goods or may be too expensive. New suppliers may not offer credit terms, so cash flow is affected as the supplier must be paid prior to delivery.

Weakness	Control proposed	Risk controlled
No checks prior to inputting the invoice onto the Excel spreadsheet are completed back to the original order or the GRN.	Compare invoices to purchase orders and GRNs to verify what was received. Review invoices for prices, quantities and calculations.	Risk that invoices may not match what was ordered or what was received.
Invoices are not logged when they arrive at CCC.	Reference invoices (stamp with sequential number and supplier reference). This will ensure that **all** invoices received go through the review and payment process.	There is a risk that invoices get missed when they arrive in the post. Company fails to pay for goods/services and loses suppliers.
Currently, CCC only pays invoices at the end of the month.	The spreadsheet should detail the terms and conditions for the invoice, and any payment terms and whether any settlement or early discount can be taken. This would be significantly easier and be an automatic procedure if CCC had accounting software instead of a manual system.	Company may miss early settlement discounts or promotions, thus paying more for inventory.
There is no mention of how CCC can prevent paying a supplier twice. The spreadsheet does not appear to be updated once the payment has been made and there is a risk that cheques could be delayed in the post and a new one written if the supplier chases for payment.	Payments should be recorded promptly in the cash book and ledger. Propose that BACS payments (which are easily traceable and quicker) are used instead of cheques.	Company pays more than once and the supplier does not correct the mistake.
Goods are only checked for damage when they arrive; they are not verified to any order number.	Verify all incoming inventory back to a purchase order or purchase order listing (this may be manual in the case of CCC). Confirm that the inventory has been received and ensure the GRN is promptly sent to the accounts office (stamping the GRN with a sequential number so that the accounting team can see whether any GRNs are missing).	There is a risk that unordered, incorrect or wrong goods are accepted upon delivery.

Weakness	Control proposed	Risk controlled
Cheques are the only method provided for CCC paying its suppliers. This can delay payment if the signatory is not available leading to the use of pre-signed cheques.	Cheques should be requisitioned and requests evidenced with supporting documentation. Cheque payments should be authorised by someone other than a signatory. Cheques should never be signed before the amount and the payee are completed. Signed cheques should be dispatched promptly.	Only make payments to the correct recipients and for the correct amounts which are authorised.
Purchase orders are not ticked off by the accounting team, so they are not aware of what invoices they are expecting. Equally, GRNs are not verified and checked against invoices received on a systematic basis. There is a risk that goods may have arrived but not be invoiced (accrual at year end missing) or an invoice has been received but no goods (in which case, the invoice should not be paid until receipt).	Purchase order listing should be regularly reviewed and any missing orders chased up. GRNs should be matched to orders and invoices matched to GRNs. GRNs should be verified and checked against invoices received on a systematic basis.	Financial statements may be misstated by recording a purchase but not inventory, or recording inventory but not the associated liability. Penalty from HMRC for recording VAT in the wrong VAT period.

Activity 8: CCC – payroll controls

Payroll control in place	Control weakness	Suggested control to be introduced
Cash wages are kept in the safe once calculated. They are handed to Jim, the showroom and marketing manager for distribution (see weakness).	Although wages should be handed out by Jim, this can be overridden if he is busy.	BACS payments to be introduced for all staff to ensure only fully validated amounts are received by staff (and fully traceable if there is a dispute). Cash wages should cease. Payslips could be posted to the home address. If cash wages are retained: • Identity of staff should be verified before payment (with wages being signed out by staff). • Distributions of cash wages should be recorded.

Payroll control in place	Control weakness	Suggested control to be introduced
Staff rotas with details of hours worked are sent by the managers to the payroll clerk.	Gross pay is calculated manually, which increases the risk of errors. There is no verification of when staff start or finish, as no time records are kept.	Introduce a payroll system which calculates gross pay based on hours worked instead of manual calculation. Regular checks should be carried out of the payroll records against the HR records and vice versa. If retaining manual system, ensure that another member of staff verifies the calculation.
Payroll clerk counts out the cash and draws up the BACS listing.	Errors can occur or additional amounts be added to the cash wages.	Segregation of duties of the calculation and payment of wages and salaries. BACS payments should be verified by management once set up on the system by the payroll clerk; however, they only agree the amount (the calculation itself is not reviewed). Bank transfer lists should be prepared and authorised. Bank transfer lists should be compared to the payroll.
Deductions are calculated by payroll clerk using tax tables (see pre-seen scenario).	Errors can occur and incorrect deductions possibly made. There is a risk that incorrect submissions are made to HMRC.	Ensure all deductions have been properly calculated and authorised. Consider outsourcing to a payroll bureau or using approved HMRC software to comply with RTI requirements.

Activity 9: Security and IT at CCC

(a) The company might put in place the following rules regarding the use and control of passwords:

- Passwords must not be written down.
- Passwords must not be shared.
- Passwords must be changed regularly.
- Passwords must not be generic.
- When a staff member leaves the company, password access must be cancelled that day.
- Password access can only be set up for new staff with management authorisation.
- Staff access to different parts of the system must be regularly reviewed.

(b) These rules and controls protect the integrity of the system and the company. If one password is used by all staff (generic), there is little point in using them, as the whole system is open to all. This lack of control then increases the risk of errors, from staff using parts of the system they are not trained to use, and fraud.

Access to the system should be controlled so that staff are not granted access to parts they do not require. If staff leave, their access should be cancelled immediately so they cannot continue to use the system, and other staff cannot use their passwords. Often, companies make sharing of passwords a disciplinary offence to ensure that controls are maintained.

(c) The policy states that only licensed software purchased by the company may be installed on company devices – however, the warehouse has two computers which have a personal version of software on them supplied by the warehouse manager.

There is no evidence of the payroll and purchase systems being regularly backed up, either to local backup devices or 'cloud' based support. It is not stated whether Stefan is using company-purchased hardware for the backup of the sales system or not. It is not evident that this is kept off site or locked away in the company safe in case of theft or fire.

Doors to the accounting department are kept open (even though there is a secure keypad-based lock) and the public can easily enter as the bathrooms are nearby.

Payroll is prepared in the same open area as the rest of the accounting function. There is a risk that secure and confidential information regarding staff salaries is open to access by other employees.

Activity 10: Ensuring ethical behaviour at work

Fundamental ethical principle	Explain how CCC may demonstrate these principles in practice
Integrity	The accounting function and system should be used to ensure information is accurate and not misleading. Staff should ensure that any issues regarding quality of data are raised immediately with management. The directors should ensure that financial statements are completed in a timely fashion.
Objectivity	Staff must not allow bias, conflict of interest or undue influence of others to override professional or business relationships or actions. This would include any judgements made regarding sums either owed by or owed to the company (eg applying more favourable terms of trade to friends than other customers would normally get).
Professional competence and due care	Ensure employees regularly update their technical knowledge, especially those with a responsibility for payroll, taxes and financial record keeping. Ensure regular monitoring of controls and processes by management so changes only occur when the business needs them. Ensure all employees are aware of the health and safety regulations at work and that they attend any relevant courses. If staff do not feel that they can adequately complete a task, or are asked to do something which they do not feel able to do, the issue should be raised with management and either an alternative resource should be found or training should be supplied.
Confidentiality	Security of payroll, supplier and customer data should be maintained. Company business should not be discussed outside of the office or with third parties. Passwords should be used and data should be kept securely, either virtually or in locked cabinets, maintaining the security of information at all times.

Fundamental ethical principle	Explain how CCC may demonstrate these principles in practice
Professional behaviour	Ensure staff remain professional and courteous to customers and suppliers and other employees. A culture should be built that enables staff to supply accurate and timely information to the best of their abilities.

Activity 11: Ethical conflicts at CCC

(1) There is an **integrity** issue here alongside a **professional competence and due care** issue. Using averages instead of actual figures will almost certainly result in an inaccurate listing, and a report prepared without 'due care'.

Stefan should report the problem to Mr Cookridge and ask for an extension to the deadline in order to provide an accurate listing.

(2) There is a **confidentiality** issue here. Margaret needs the customer's authority to disclose the information; she may also need to confirm the identity of the person making the request. She should also take steps to protect the security of the information when she sends it – eg not using email (which can be intercepted), and stating clearly that the information is confidential.

There is also a **professional behaviour** issue: to comply with the Data Protection Regulations, it is likely that CCC has rules about what to do on receipt of such a request.

Margaret should not divulge any information without confirming with a manager that she is legally allowed to do so.

(3) There are issues of **professional competence and due care** here. Stefan is not qualified to give advice on matters of taxation. Even if he were qualified, any answer he gives on the spot would risk being incomplete or inaccurate, potentially causing his friend tax losses. Stefan should advise his friend that he is unable to help, and point her in the direction of a qualified tax accountant.

(4) There is an **objectivity** issue here as the gift is of significant value. Think about how it looks. A third-party observer is entitled to wonder what 'special favours' deserve this extra reward – and/or how such a gift may influence Stefan when making payments to the supplier in future. Stefan should politely decline the offer, pointing out that he is merely doing his job.

Activity 12: How systems and procedures support sustainability practices

Sustainability in the flooring industry

Manufacturers may decide to adopt the following initiatives:

- The invention of longer-lasting flooring products
- The use of more sustainable materials in flooring products

Product development will require an understanding of the costs involved in order to accurately reflect them within the financial statements. IAS 38 *Intangible assets* requires a distinction between the costs associated with pure research (which must be expensed) and development work (which leads to the creation of an intangible asset which is then amortised when the associated product goes into production).

In addition, certain criteria need to be fulfilled for the costs to be recognised – eg that the amounts involved can be realistically measured and that funds exist for the satisfactory completion of the development work.

Both of these require an accounting system that is able to generate the necessary information that supports accurate decision making (both internally for the manufacturer and externally for stakeholders using the company's financial statements). There will also be underpinning procedures (eg budgetary control information and cash-flow forecasts) that support the achievement of these sustainability practices.

Sustainability in other contexts

In some cases, **external reporting** to support sustainable practices requires information that is extracted from the accounting system (eg financial information relevant to sustainability-related risks and opportunities).

Government grants are often awarded for pursuing sustainable initiatives but usually require evidence of sustainable expenditure before they can be claimed. Such evidence is usually available in the form of invoices, contracts and payments, all of which are accessed via an organisation's accounting system and underpinning processes.

In addition, so-called '**green bonds**' are available from commercial lenders for organisations to borrow at advantageous rates of interest but only if they can demonstrate that they are investing in technology that is considered sustainable. Evidence for this usually takes the form of invoices and other similar documentation.

Sustainable internal reporting can also benefit from the use of information obtained from an organisation's accounting system and underpinning procedures. Take the example of a company buying and selling both new and used electric vehicles. There may be interested in pursuing a number of key sustainability practices (eg managing their energy usage and supporting their customers with the transition to a low carbon drive) which require information obtained from these systems and procedures.

The accounting system and underpinning processes may also **identify information that points towards a future the organisation is not yet prepared for**. Take the example of a company whose products require certain natural resources that are either considered scarce (eg water in the manufacture of clothing) or unsustainable (eg coal used in the manufacture of steel). Analysis of an organisation's dependence on these resources can help to identify constraints that need to be addressed if the organisation wishes to pursue more sustainable practices.

Tutorial note. Other sensible points relevant to your context would be appropriate. Just remember to explain how each sustainability practice is being supported by the relevant part of the account system and its underpinning process.

Test your learning

1 An accounting system should meet the expectations and requirements of the organisation.

Required

Select the key objectives of the accounting system from the options below.

Tick ALL that apply.

	✓
Cost effectiveness	
Ease of use	
Reliable	
Providing timely information	

2 **Complete the following statement.**

The requirement for an accountant to act diligently is part of the fundamental principle of

[▼] .

Picklist

- Integrity
- Objectivity
- Professional behaviour
- Professional competence and due care

3 **Complete the following statement:**

Management should regularly ensure that staff perform [▼] of the receivables ledger to ensure accuracy and completeness of the data.

Picklist

- Assessments
- Inspections
- Reconciliations
- Teeming and lading

4 **Complete the following statement:**

Control objectives in relation to taking orders and extending credit are part of the

[▼] system of the accounting system.

Picklist

- Payroll
- Purchases
- Sales

5 **Complete the following statement:**

Completion of GRNs is a control activity related to the control objective of [▼].

Picklist

- Ensuring goods and services received are used for the company's purposes
- Only accepting goods and services that have been ordered and appropriately authorised
- Only accepting goods received that are of a sufficient quantity for the purposes of the organisation
- Recording all money received

6 **Which of the following payroll controls would help to ensure that payroll payments are accurate?**

	Would help	Would not help
The payroll clerk manually recalculates all their own work to confirm the accuracy of the payroll.	O	O
Wages are automatically calculated by the payroll system which takes the number of hours worked by each employee from their swipe-card data and applies an hourly rate that is part of the system's master files.	O	O
The total amount payable for each month's payroll is reviewed and authorised for payment by the chief accountant.	O	O

4 Making changes

Learning outcomes

4.2	**Analyse the implications of changes to the accounting system** Students need to be able to: • Quantify the costs of recommendations, stating assumptions made • Undertake a cost benefit analysis • Evaluate the implications of the changes to operating procedures and time spent • Review recommendations against ethical and sustainability principles, including social, corporate and environmental issues • Undertake a SWOT analysis.

Assessment context

The topics covered in this chapter could be included in Task 1, Task 3 or Task 4 of the Role Scenario Assessment, which test your understanding of ethics and accounting fundamentals, the management accounting process and internal control systems respectively.

Qualification context

This chapter builds on content that you will have seen in your previous studies and will complement what you have learned at Level 4 in both Management Accounting and Financial Statements.

Business context

Management should regularly review the accounting system for relevance and to ensure that it is working as originally intended. As businesses grow and change, so should the accounting systems within them, therefore management is responsible for ensuring that regular review is undertaken.

Systemic weaknesses in accounting systems require changes to be made, otherwise the potential for exposure to fraud and error increases. Any system changes need to be thoroughly evaluated to ensure they deliver a value for money solution.

Changes made to the accounting system must be carefully planned and controls put in place to ensure that the business can continue during the time of transition.

Chapter overview

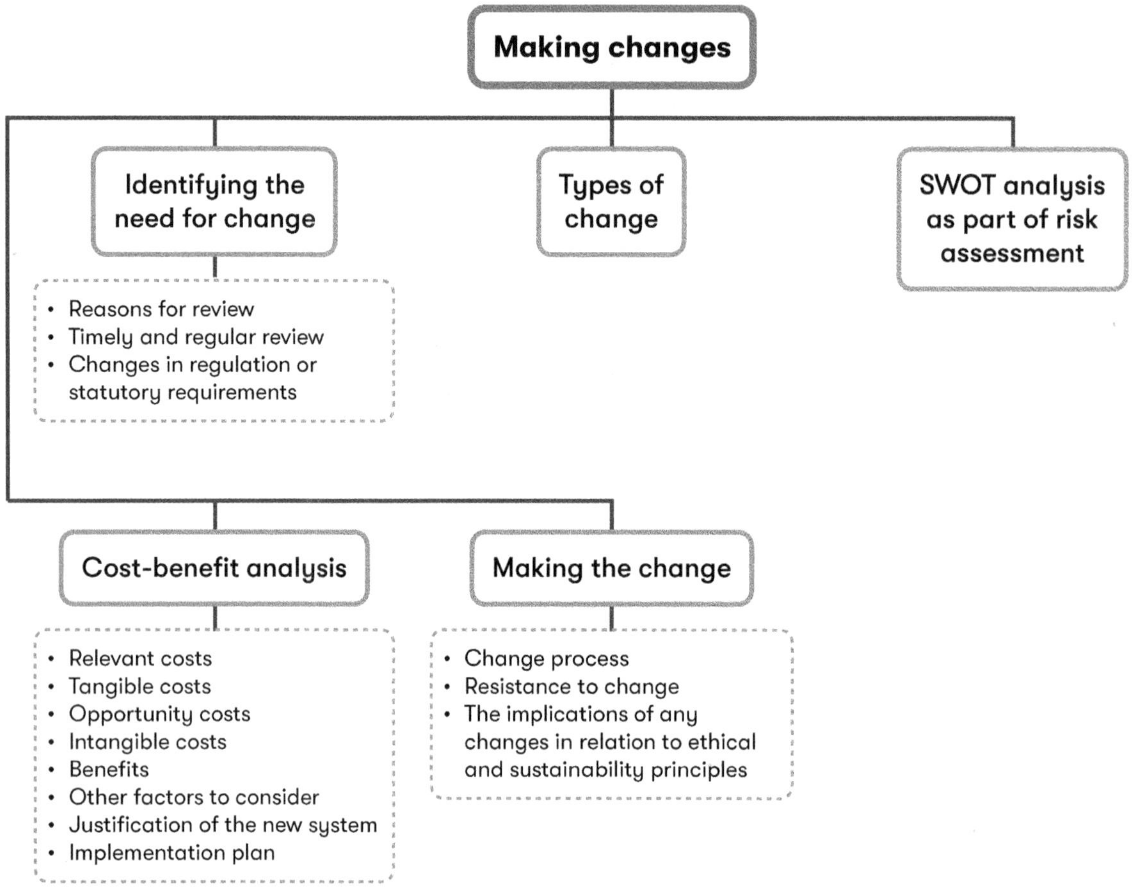

Introduction

This chapter looks at what happens when organisations consider making changes to their accounting system and internal controls.

Before any changes are made, analysis of the existing systems should be carried out to identify what changes are necessary. **SWOT** can be used to identify changes needed to the accounting system.

To ensure any planned changes generate benefits, the preparation of a **cost benefit analysis** should be undertaken. This helps management identify and understand all of the relevant costs associated with implementing system changes, and the benefits that will be gained from doing so.

Costs and benefits may be **tangible**, meaning that they can be quantified, or **intangible**, meaning they are harder to assess, as they cannot be quantified in monetary terms.

Included in any analysis should be the **opportunity costs** of any actions, eg if money is spent on a new system, you should consider where else this could be spent within the organisation (sales promotions or new product development).

Aside from the financial aspects, it will also be important to assess the impact that any proposed changes will have on staff and other stakeholders.

1 Identifying the need for change

In the previous chapters of this Course Book, we have identified situations where change may be needed in an accounting system or a system of internal controls. The need for change can sometimes become apparent when deploying many of the tools we have seen previously – eg fraud matrices, ratios and scorecards.

1.1 Reasons for review

Management often has specific reasons to undertake detailed reviews of accounting systems:

Reason	Examples
Personnel changes	Changes in management or departments Department mergers or changes (eg launching a new range of products or diversification) Rapid hiring of staff to meet demand High turnover of staff
Company strategy change	Change in focus for the company strategy Acquisition of a new business (eg in a merger or takeover) or sale of a business sector
Technology changes	New software or hardware Changes in cyber security (possibly as a result of a cyber-attack or the threat of one) or the adoption of AI
Financial reasons	Areas identified as requiring cost reduction Development of a new market for the product (eg overseas) Analysis of costs highlighting adverse ratios with similar companies in the same industry

1.2 Timely and regular review

Even if there are no specific reasons to prompt a review of the accounting systems, policies and controls, the systems should still be reviewed on a timely basis.

Often, there may be small, incremental changes which are not significant enough to generate a full review of the system – eg a replacement head of department. (There is still a supervisor, and the systems are still working as before.) However, over time, these small changes may cause an accounting system to be less effective, less efficient or no longer fit for purpose.

Reason	Examples
Changes occurring over time	Additional stages in the process – eg additional authorising staff to cover more purchasing Changes in authorisation levels to reflect current spending Alteration of the holiday approval process to spread 'peak periods' more fairly across staff (no longer first come, first served) Monthly invoice payment runs changed to weekly Weekly paid staff to be paid monthly Moving from cash payments to staff to online banking for salaries and expenses
Post-implementation review	A new system requires changes to improve it The process of reviewing new systems once they are 'up and running' elicits further changes

Reason	Examples
Efficiencies	Efficiencies may be identified which can reduce cost, waste or time (and potentially fraud): • Using online banking instead of cheques • E-receipts instead of paper • Online ordering process instead of telephone based
Identifying problems before they occur	The current system may be working, but it may be flawed. How does it work in practice compared to how it looks on paper? There may be steps required by overworked line managers which can be shared, automated or changed. If the current system is open to neglect or abuse, problems may occur. A pre-emptive review of key areas may highlight areas for revision.

1.3 Changes in regulation or statutory requirements

Management needs to ensure that it complies with all existing regulatory requirements – however, it is also essential that it keeps abreast of any future regulatory changes which may affect the organisation.

Accounting standards change on a regular basis, and occasionally these changes will also affect the information that the organisation will be required to provide. For instance, IFRS 15 *Revenue from Contracts with Customers* requires companies to provide additional information regarding the costing and contractual revenue on long-term contracts. In this example, the company will need to ensure that this additional information is constantly updated to avoid leaving itself with a huge task at year end. Management will need to ensure that their monthly reporting is robust enough to supply the information required at year end, and to avoid any 'shocks' when the financial results are published.

Other changes which have affected organisations in recent years include:

- **Online RTI payroll reporting** to HMRC regarding payroll payments and deductions made to staff
- Revised **money laundering regulations**, increasing the checks and measures that a company must perform on new staff
- Revised **waste management regulations** and increased requirements regarding disposal and recycling
- Updates to **data protection legislation** for employees, customers and other stakeholders

An organisation must therefore have an eye on future developments and ensure that changes are not left until the last minute.

Activity 1: Business regulations

Use the information provided on CCC.

Required

(a) Consider the potential weaknesses in the organisation's ability to keep up to date and have a 'long-term view' on potential changes which may affect it.

(b) Make any recommendations for improvement, relevant to the scenario.

2 Types of change

The type of change required can be assessed by analysing:

(a) The **seriousness of the problem** to be resolved – changing a system riddled with inherent weaknesses or subject to fraud is evidently a much bigger job than ensuring an upgrade of an existing off-the-shelf payroll package.

(b) The **scope of the change** – implementing a completely new accounting system is more of a challenge than revising the responsibilities of two members of staff.

(c) The **context** in which change takes place – changes needed to safeguard jobs may be easier to implement than those that staff perceive to be cosmetic in nature, or unnecessary.

The degree of change can be classified as the following:

KEY TERM

Transformational change: A wholesale change – eg integrating all accounting functions at a centralised location with a new computer system.

Incremental change: A small change or a big change made in small steps eg gradually moving each sub-system onto an integrated accounting package.

The type of change will depend on what the **issues** are and how management decides to proceed with the changes. The need for change may be due to a **weakness** that has been identified as part of the overall process of **managing the risks** that the organisation is facing. Let's consider one of the techniques used to evaluate these risks.

3 SWOT analysis as part of risk assessment

KEY TERM

Risk assessment process: An evaluation of the risks to the achievement of the organisation's objectives.

SWOT analysis: A way for management to highlight the key issues, and review where the organisation has strengths and weaknesses and to consider any opportunities or threats, from internal and external sources.

A useful tool for analysing the accounting and internal control system, as part of the **risk assessment process**, is a SWOT analysis. SWOT stands for:

- **S**trengths
- **W**eaknesses
- **O**pportunities
- **T**hreats

The strengths and weaknesses of a system will be **internal** factors.

Once strengths and weaknesses have been identified, recommendations can be made to address the weaknesses.

Opportunities and threats are **external** to the actual system itself.

In these instances, management need to consider how they can use these external opportunities (eg market conditions) or mitigate against potential threats (eg changes in legislation, interest rate changes).

A SWOT analysis is a way for management to highlight the key issues; however, it is important that they focus on only a few at a time as proposing too many changes may be detrimental to staff morale, confusing to customers or clients, or expensive to implement in terms of time and financial outlay.

Activity 2: SWOT analysis

Use the information you have received so far in respect of CCC.

Required

Complete a SWOT analysis for CCC using the format below, focusing on the strengths and weaknesses of the accounting systems, and the opportunities and threats for the company as a whole.

Strengths	Weaknesses

Opportunities	Threats

4 Cost-benefit analysis

A cost-benefit analysis takes **recommendations** for changes and improvements in the accounting system and its controls and **analyses** them in terms of the costs and benefits to the company of implementing them.

Change should be **cost-effective** in that the benefits of the change should outweigh its costs.

Both **costs** and **benefits** can be **tangible** and **intangible**.

KEY TERM

> **Cost-benefit analysis:** Analyses recommendations for change in terms of the costs and benefits to the company of implementing them.

A simple **cost-benefit analysis** may look something like this:

	£'000	£'000
Initial costs		
Cost of machinery	500	
Staff training	75	
Site preparation	10	
		585
Annual running costs		
Safety checks (required every 2,100 hours of production)	150	
Replacement drill heads	14	
		164
Total costs over lifetime (5 years)		749
Savings		
Staff hours savings	25	
Costs of running the old machinery (5 × 155)	775	
		800
Total net benefit over 5 years		51

In order to produce an accurate and meaningful cost-benefit analysis, it is necessary to ensure all relevant costs and benefits are included.

4.1 Relevant costs

These are costs that are relevant to any potential decision to change something. If something is not relevant, it does not need to be included in any cost/benefit analysis (eg costs that have already been incurred before a decision is made).

An organisation may also decide that it is more efficient or economical to outsource a service or a department. For example, CCC may decide that it is better to utilise outside expertise, albeit at an additional finance cost, in order to run and maintain the payroll and HR function. This would need to be compared with the current cost of providing the service in-house.

Refer to your Level 4 Management Accounting materials if you need to refresh your knowledge on this area.

4.2 Tangible costs

KEY TERM

> **Tangible costs:** Identified, quantifiable costs of the change eg buying a new software package.

Tangible costs are relatively easy to value as they can be quantified in terms of time and/or money.

Illustration 1: Tangible costs

The tangible costs of a recommended new computer system are the quantifiable cost of:

- The system itself (training, hardware and software)
- The loss of staff time while they are training
- Software licences
- Future upgrades to maintain speed of processing or due to technical updates regarding regulation or other changes

Activity 3: Tangible cost of a new system

CCC has decided to investigate using an accountancy software package called KashCade.

There are three part-time staff in the accounting department, and they are considering adding a full-time member. The directors cannot decide how they will ensure staff are adequately trained. They are also considering whether the warehouse team and the sales team will require system access too. The estimated cost of the sales team being away for a day is expected to be £2,000 in lost sales, with the total cost of using temporary staff in the accounts team whilst they undergo training of £540 (per day).

CCC have used an external consultant (at a cost of £750) who has estimated that the increase in efficiencies will save CCC £6,300 per year. This is in addition to the expected increase in sales (of £5,000 for the first year, increasing by 15% each year) due to the ability to make online sales and reduce inventory holding and tying up cash.

KashCade has broken down the elements of the system as follows:

> Dear Sirs/Madams,
>
> Thank you for your interest in our integrated accounting system. We are happy to provide you with details of the following:
>
> **Basic system 1 (cloud)**, which includes:
>
> - Receivables ledger system, including pre-numbered invoices and aged debt reports
> - Payables ledger system, incorporating purchase orders which can be matched against incoming invoices. Inventory aging reports are included.
> - General ledger and summary trial balance reports
> - Journal functionality
> - Exception reporting
> - Budget input and comparison tools
> - Updates and upgrades occur regularly and will be automated at no extra cost

Additional add-ons which can be purchased:

- Payroll function which will also integrate with the general ledger and allow full real time information (RTI) to HM Revenue & Customs, as well as year-end reporting and payslip production
- Draft financial statements reporting
- Advanced inventory option which allocates a FIFO cost and monitors the current inventory cost, allocating costs to allow a 'cost of project' for each customer

Annual costs

	Initial costs	Annual costs
Basic system 1 (cloud)	£5,000 (to cover assistance with data migration)	£3,250 (up to 10 licensed users)
Payroll	–	£550
Financial accounts	–	£750
Advanced inventory	-	£1,250

We also recommend using our training partner, Best Practical Performance Ltd, to supply the training to staff on the KashCade system.

In-house training (maximum of 15 people) 2 days	£3,500
Course at local college (3 days)	£350 per person
Online course (completed in own time)	£75 per person (license limited to access for six months)

We can include a full support system, 24 hours a day by remote operators, for £250 per year, with the first year free of charge.

If you have any further questions, please do not hesitate to contact us.

Yours sincerely,

P. Bryan

Sales director Kash Cade Ltd

Required

Prepare a report showing a brief financial cost-benefit analysis of taking the full package including add-ons, together with additional narrative. Ensure that the following have been included in your report:

(a) **Identify the tangible costs of this purchasing decision.**

(b) **Estimate the overall costs of purchasing this software. Consider also how CCC could reduce these costs, and the implications of doing so.**

4.3 Opportunity costs

An **opportunity cost** is the value of an activity that has not taken place, because of a decision to do something else. For example, if a taxi driver is offered a £100 fare for a two-hour round trip to the airport, they would need to factor in the cost of any regular fares they will lose as a result. If the taxi driver normally makes £30 an hour in regular fares, the opportunity cost of the airport run is £60, leaving them with an effective benefit of £40 – lower than the £100 fare offered.

Wherever possible, any opportunity costs of making a particular change should be included in the cost-benefit analysis.

4.4 Intangible costs

KEY TERM

Intangible costs: Cannot be quantified in financial terms, where the costs of the change are more difficult to identify and quantify – eg the cost of lost custom as customers go elsewhere during the disruption caused by the change.

Activity 4: Intangible costs

Consider the new computer system and training programme proposed to CCC in the previous activity.

Required

Discuss the intangible costs which may impact the decisions of CCC management on whether to go ahead with the new system, and deciding on which training programme to be undertaken.

4.5 Benefits

There should be at least some tangible and/or intangible benefits of any changes made to the accounting system, otherwise there is no point making them.

KEY TERM

Tangible benefits: May be more difficult to quantify than tangible costs, but easy to identify (eg less time spent creating invoices, improved efficiency).

Intangible benefits: Benefits of the change that are more difficult to identify and quantify, eg improved reputation for efficiency, improving the customer experience in a showroom, facilitating an increase in the amount of time spent browsing, or making conditions for staff better so that they are more motivated at work.

It may not be possible to put estimated values against every benefit, especially intangible ones, but describing the benefits clearly is extremely important in a cost-benefit analysis. These often form powerful arguments in favour of implementing a recommendation.

A systems change may be due to the availability of a new software package, improving the information which is available to management from the raw data input by the employees. This can increase staff morale, as they are able to work more efficiently or may benefit from the automation of mundane manual tasks. A new system may offer new opportunities for retention of customers or attracting new customers, such as loyalty programmes or bonuses for referring friends to the company.

Activity 5: Benefits of training

Consider again the training discussed in the earlier activity.

Required

What intangible benefits might there be in sending CCC's staff on the training programme?

4.6 Other factors to consider

Aside from the costs and benefits already discussed in this chapter, there are other considerations which will impact how an organisation approaches a potential change or assesses whether it is necessary to change or not.

Using a **SWOT analysis** can help to focus management's attention on the areas that need developing, eg improving customer service or reducing wastage in a manufacturing process.

Where risks have been identified in completing a **fraud matrix** (Chapter 2), management can use this information to tailor any changes to the system so as to mitigate the most significant risks. This will ensure that changes are focused in the most cost-efficient and effective manner.

Once a decision has been made on the basis of **costs, benefits and risks**, both from an operational and strategic view, there are further points to consider.

It is vital that any changes made during the transition are 'future proof' as far as possible. For example, any software should be able to cope with new accounting standards or reporting requirements already planned for implementation.

It should also meet the latest regulatory and legal requirements. It is important to ensure that any transitioning or changes to the system or accounting function are carefully controlled and monitored by management, with timely reviews to avoid costly mistakes or hurried remedial action.

4.7 Justification of the new system

Now that we have considered the individual elements of the cost-benefit analysis, it is necessary to present the information in a way which is accessible to the decision makers.

It is essential that a clear rationale is provided to support the requirement for change, and that potential issues have been identified as far as possible, with suggestions for actions to mitigate these risks.

Assessment focus point

Ensure that your recommendations (and highlighted risks) are relevant to the scenario you are given. Use the information provided to keep your answers concise and relevant to the question being asked. Do not ignore recommendations if the question asks for risks and recommendations. Consider your audience: is it the management, owners of the business or the staff?

4.8 Implementation plan

The most important part of the change process will be the detail behind the implementation plan.

This often includes the rationale behind the decision making as well as the main budgetary elements, such as the cost of the consultancy, the costs of new software and computers or other equipment. Contingency costs may be built into the plan, especially where riskier or trickier areas may be taking place – eg extra costs for training, testing of the new system or installation in remote branches of the organisation.

The aim is to give a best view of the main issues and where the costs are to be spent.

The plan should not only cover financial costs, but also consider the morale of staff – including when to inform them of the changes, how often to update them and how this can be best be carried out.

Activity 6: Cost-benefit analysis

Use the information you have been provided with to date, including the answers to the activities in this chapter.

(1) Assume that the software will initially be used for five years.

(2) Where the information regarding the actual cost cannot be defined (due to insufficient available information), show how it may be an issue in the narrative to your report.

(3) Think of costs not just in terms of money spent but also in relation to time and any other quantifiable measure.

(4) Where you cannot quantify either costs or benefits, you should indicate with '£X' within the analysis where a quantified cost or benefit could be determined.

Required

Prepare a detailed cost-benefit report for the two directors which provides an analysis for implementing a centralised, integrated accounting system in CCC, with appropriate staff training.

5 Making the change

There are various factors which should be reflected on by management when considering the process for change within an organisation.

5.1 Change process

The main elements of the change process can be described in the following flow chart.

Evaluate

- Evaluate the system and its problems – determine that the particular change required is actually necessary eg is there a regulatory change that requires a system update? Systems should be evaluated prior to proposing any recommendations.
- If a system is working sufficiently well, it may mean that the recommended change is not required.

↓

Recommend

- Proposal of a solution to the identified problem
- Consider any previous attempts to correct problems and mitigate for possible issues (busy seasons, such as year end, Christmas, holiday periods, availability of key personnel)
- Expertise: Are experts or contractors required to assist with the implementation (or even additional staff to help out with day to day roles when key staff are involved in the implementation?)

↓

Communication

- Clear communication of the proposed changes to all relevant stakeholders, including users of the new systems and those who receive information (such as monthly reports) from it
- Give a rationale behind the change and the reasons for it
- Explain when and how the changes will take place
- Consider any feedback and whether plans may need to be adjusted accordingly
- Agreed change initially takes longer, as everyone has to 'buy in' to it, but it can be faster overall than forced change as residual resistance is generally lower once the new system is implemented.

↓

Training

- Staff will need to be trained on the new system, this may be new software or adapting to the new policies and procedures to be put in place
- Consider how staff will be trained to ensure they are familiar with the new system, but minimise disruption to the main business of the organisation

↓

Implementation

- Draw up a timetable for change
- Consider running systems side by side for a period to ensure no disruption to the business
- Consider whether all precautions been taken to ensure there are no 'gaps' which may be opportunities for system failure, potential fraud or loss of information

↓

Review

- Review the effectiveness of the change – has the problem identified been remedied as intended? You may need to make further changes if not.

Figure 4.1: Flowchart of the change process

5.2 Resistance to change

Individuals working within a system tend to put up **barriers to change** (eg objecting, staging a 'go slow', disputing every detail, etc), even when the change is perfectly valid and even when it is quite small. This is because most people **fear** change, or rather they fear the uncertainty that surrounds change.

Managers need to be aware of these concerns, and think about how best to **overcome** the inevitable resistance they will face when planning system changes.

With any proposed and significant change, it is advisable to **communicate** the reasons and discuss with staff why the change is happening, eg discussions with trade unions, staff representatives, regular updates (email or face-to-face).

Activity 7: Issues during transition

The directors of CCC have decided to investigate how to improve the computer and reporting systems of the accounts team. They are considering the following proposals:

(1) The introduction of an integrated accounting system which will require new training for everyone who uses it, including warehouse staff and sales staff

(2) Strict reporting deadlines regarding aged receivables reporting and high-level monthly management accounts

(3) Recruiting a full-time senior qualified accountant to oversee the accounting function

Required

Identify any problems which may arise at CCC when implementing any of the above proposals.

5.3 The implications of any changes in relation to ethical and sustainability principles

We have already discussed that any recommended changes to the accounting system need to be evaluated in terms of their implications. In addition to those based on costs and benefits, organisations also need to consider these implications in both **ethical** and **sustainability terms**, taking **social**, **corporate** and **environmental** issues into account.

Activity 8: CCC new accounting system

CCC is also considering the adoption of a different cloud-based accounting system to replace the existing system of standalone PCs. This will require new hardware including the installation of a server at CCC to process transactions which is expected to be compatible with other systems around the business. The supplier of the new system has guaranteed that up to 20% of existing costs could be saved if CCC implements this new system due to being able to use additional spare capacity on existing servers used by their other clients.

Staff will be expected to undertake training in how to use the new system, which uses digital dashboards instead of paper-based reporting. It is expected that the core times when the additional spare capacity on external servers is available will be between 2pm and 10pm during the week. Currently, no dedicated project manager at CCC has been appointed yet to take responsibility for the transition to the new system.

One of key selling features for the new accounting system is an artificial intelligence (AI) driven sales ledger which will make decisions on credit scores for new and existing customers.

Required

Evaluate the proposed new accounting system at CCC using the following categories:

- **Ethical**
- **Sustainable**
- **Social**
- **Corporate**
- **Environmental**

Chapter summary

- Change may be needed to an accounting system because it contains systemic weaknesses that make it prone to fraud and error.
- In other cases, change may be necessary due to factors within the organisation, the period of time since any previous changes and any legal or regulatory issues.
- A change may be transformational or incremental.
- The degree of change necessary depends on the seriousness of the problem, the scope of the change and the context in which the change will take place.
- The management of an organisation may well perform a SWOT to assess the risks associated with change management.
- A cost-benefit analysis will enable management to assess the level of change required and whether an alternative option may be preferred.
- To numerically analyse the decision to proceed with a decision (shutdown, make or buy decisions), the relevant costs of a project should be evaluated.
- Costs and benefits may be tangible, such as improved efficiencies, improved customer service or decreased operational costs. These tangible costs can be measured.
- The intangible costs and benefits are harder to quantify, such as improved employee morale due to a better working environment.
- The prospect of change can meet with resistance from employees, management, shareholders or customers. It is vital that the expectations and fears of these stakeholders are considered and mitigated in advance of any change occurring.
- The transition from one system to another should be planned and controlled to ensure no loss of data and to minimise disruption to the organisation, its employees and customers.
- Implementation needs to be evaluated in relation to ethical and sustainability practices – including those of a social, corporate and environmental nature.

Activity answers

Activity 1: Business regulations

(a) Potential weaknesses

- Lack of qualified accountancy staff and no evidence of ongoing professional development from the payroll clerk suggest that CCC may not be aware of any accounting or payroll developments. Evidence suggests that CCC may already be in breach of the requirement to provide a pension to staff (although it is not explicit that CCC has breached any deadline).
- There does not appear to be any nominated officer (in line with money laundering regulations) within CCC. It is doubtful that all of the regulations are being followed correctly and staff have no central point to discuss any concerns in this area.
- There is no evidence of health and safety checks; this may be an issue with the company insurance if there is an accident at work.
- Data protection breaches have already been identified, but staff have not been trained in this area so further breaches are likely to occur.

(b) Recommendations

- Ensure that management review the training of staff regarding companies regulations, especially in money laundering, health and safety, etc.
- Designate different members of staff to become the 'champions' in those areas, providing training and ensuring that these members of staff take the time to inform the rest of the team. This should also improve morale as the staff will feel motivated that CCC is investing in their training and valuing their input on these important areas.
- Ensure that Stefan, Sonja and any new accountancy staff regularly attend update courses and request that they report back on any new developments to the management team so that they have a view of what systems or processes may need to be amended at the earliest opportunity.

Activity 2: SWOT analysis

Strengths	Weaknesses
• An open plan accounts office ensures that when staff are in and working with each other, they can communicate freely and cover each other's work when absent. • The cheque book is kept in a locked desk in the office (but see weaknesses). • A credit reference agency is used to decide whether to grant credit to new customers. • Some credit control procedures are in place. • Controls over cheques coming into the office involve a manual day book then accounts. • Staff seem keen to improve systems – the accounts receivable clerk has implemented some initiatives. • Cash movement is reduced by using cash to make up wages.	• As most accounts staff are part time, there are often occasions when no one is in the office. The door is generally propped open; there is a risk members of the public could access the office. • As all staff can access the office and the accounting system with common passwords, there is a lack of control. There will also be issues concerning communication between staff as they are not all in the office at the same time. • Stand-alone computers, with no central system or database, reduce the ability to produce meaningful reports for key stakeholders. There is a risk of loss of data if a computer fails. • Staff as a whole are not qualified in accounting, which poses a risk of errors, exacerbated by the relaxed controls and also a lack of accountability.

Strengths	Weaknesses
	• Suppliers are paid by cheque – the frequent use of cheques can lead to the risk of cheques being stolen and fraudulently used. • Manual calculation of weekly payroll with no secondary review is a weakness as it can lead to errors or fraudulent increases in staff pay. • Wages are paid in cash – any use of cash poses a risk of theft. • Overdue debts are often not followed up beyond an initial phone call. • The cheque book is kept in an easily accessible drawer which is sometimes left unlocked. • Staff are not trained in Excel, increasing the risk of errors. • Invoices are produced using Word. This has the potential for errors, such as duplication of invoice number or incorrectly calculated. • Cash is not counted when removed from the tills on weekdays. • No controls over petty cash and over cash taken from tills. • No contingency planning – accounting staff are not able to take on each other's roles when absent. • No control on authorisation of payments to suppliers – signing of blank cheques to cover absence. • Payments to suppliers are made without checking systems or informing other staff. • Lack of controls on staff hours may lead to incorrect rotas and staff pay. • Pay packets for more than one pay period can be stored onsite. This is a weakness as too much cash is in the office. • Unclaimed pay packets left in employee's drawer (risk of theft).

Opportunities	Threats
• There is an opportunity to use one central accounting system on networked computers, which will ensure there is better cover for work when staff are absent and better reporting of key financial information to relevant stakeholders. • There is an opportunity to train staff in accounting and also in the systems they use, making them much more aware of the controls and procedures they should be operating and also be more efficient. • There is an opportunity to train staff in each other's roles – perhaps with a backup member of staff for each. This could motivate staff and also ensure cover during absence. • There is an opportunity to re-outsource the payroll function to the company's accountants. • The obvious opportunity to remove a large amount of fraud risk is to switch to non-cash transactions where possible (eg all staff and suppliers should be paid via bank transfer and customers allowed to use card payments or bank transfer instead of cash and cheques)	• The use of one common password is a threat to systems and the data held within them (eg through unauthorised access or malware deployed externally). • The lack of formal procedures and controls has contributed to extensive use of the overdraft facility and caused the bank concern. This is a cash flow threat to the company if the bank requires this to be repaid. • There appears to be no backup taken of the current systems. This is a threat because key financial data would be lost if the systems failed or a cybersecurity event occurred. • Regulatory environment is constantly changing, eg potential changes to VAT rates. The accounting system needs to be able to recognise these changes and react accordingly. • Debt collection – while a relationship with a debt collection agency is in place, this is rarely used due to the costs involved. This may mean that debts are never recovered.

Activity 3: Tangible cost of a new system

(a) The tangible costs associated with the new system might include:

- Initial cost of implementing the new system
- Ongoing annual costs
- Cost of lost staff time for training, if this is quantifiable
- Cost of lost productive staff time, if staff are used to preparing the data for migration to the new system and assisting the software contractors, if this is quantifiable

(b) Cost of implementing the new system:

	£
Initial costs	
Basic system 1	5,000
Training costs	3,500
	8,500
Ongoing annual costs	
Basic system 1	3,250
Add-ons	2,550
	5,800

These costs would be reduced if CCC decides not to go ahead with all of the add-ons – however, having an integrated system would lead to reduced calculation errors, simpler and faster online reporting (to HMRC for PAYE) and closer monitoring of the inventory chain.

- Initial training costs will be dependent on how many staff will be trained. If at least ten staff members (including both directors) are trained, it would be cost effective to have an in-house training programme. The financial outlay would be the same as sending all ten to college, but it would reduce the travel expenses and would be more likely to tailor the learning experience of the staff.
- The downside would be that ten people would be unavailable to perform business work on the day of training.
- CCC may consider sending selected members of staff to college to complete the learning (eg five staff members costing £350 each; total cost of £1,750) and these staff could act as 'champions' and assist those members of staff who will complete the online training (eg more restricted users, maybe in the warehouse).

The training programme selected will need to be considered in terms of the financial costs, plus the opportunity costs of staff being unavailable to process orders to secure sales.

	£
Basic system 1 – initial cost	5,000
In-house training (most cost effective for ten members of staff)	3,500
Basic system 1 – annual cost	3,250

Activity 4: Intangible costs

Intangible costs might include:

- The cost of the 'learning curve' whereby staff will be slower initially on the new software whilst they practise using it. There may initially be teething problems, eg being able to use the reports and understanding what the system can and cannot do.
- Customer dissatisfaction at potential shop closure, or restricted access to staff during the period of transition and training.

Activity 5: Benefits of training

Intangible benefits might include:

- Staff are better trained in basic knowledge and skills so they are more efficient.
- Staff morale improves as they feel valued due to the investment in training them, increasing their motivation.
- Customers see well-trained and knowledgeable staff so the company's reputation is enhanced, leading to more repeat custom and recommendations from satisfied customers.
- If everyone is trained at the same time (eg using the in-house training), staff can discuss issues with each other rather than struggling on alone. It will act as a team building exercise and improve morale.

Activity 6: Cost-benefit analysis

A cost-benefit analysis of the recommendation to implement a centralised, integrated accounting system, and to train staff appropriately on it, has been completed as follows:

To: The Directors of CCC Ltd

Date: 23 April 20X3

Cost-benefit analysis on the proposed implementation of the KashCade system and staff training

	£	£
Initial costs		
Initial installation and set up	5,000	
First year's licence £(550 + 3,250 + 750 + 1,250)	5,800	
Training costs (two-day option)	3,500	
Disruption to sales and accounts department (£540 × 2) + sales department (£2,000 × 2)	5,080	
		19,380
Ongoing costs		
Support system (4 × £250)	1,000	
Annual licence (4 × £5,800)	23,200	
		24,200
Total costs		43,580
Savings		
Efficiencies due to new system £6,300 × 5		31,500
Increase in revenue/savings due to reduced inventory holding £(5,000 + 5,750 + 6,612 + 7,604 + 8,745)		33,711
Total savings		65,211
Total benefit		21,631

Costs

Set-up and annual system costs

An example of a system that would suit CCC's needs is a centralised accounting software package (eg KashCade in this example), which has been specifically created for small to medium-sized businesses. There are many similar packages on the market and a full investigation should be completed to determine which best suits the company.

A reputable, proven package with a multi-user licence would cost approximately £10,800 (including the initial set-up costs of £5,000 and the first year's licence of £5,800). The basis for choosing the package should include ease of use (eg drop-down menus), the help facility and the user manuals. The ongoing annual cost for licences will be £5,800 per year (£3,250 + £550 + £750 + £1,250), although there may be increases in future years due to inflation or upgrades in the level of cover required by CCC.

Support package costs

CCC would also need to purchase an appropriate support package to ensure users have access to trained support professionals and that software upgrades and bug fixes are received. An estimated cost for this is an additional £250 per year, although KashCade have included the first year free of charge.

Training for staff cost

Appropriate training for staff is required. If the accounting package purchased is one in common use, CCC will be able to purchase places on open courses for staff, costing approximately £350 per staff member. CCC might also consider a tailored training course for all staff at once, to include partial set-up of the system for CCC's use, which would cost approximately £3,500 and staff would be trained over two days minimising disruption to the business. Costs of replacement staff in the accounts department would be £540 per day (totalling £1,080).

There would be an opportunity cost when staff attend the training in that they would not be available to complete their work at CCC while they are on the course. This would be shown as potential lost revenue of £2,000 per day from the sales staff (totalling £4,000).

Hardware and infrastructure cost

The company requires the appropriate equipment to network the computers. This could be completed either by cable or on a secure wireless network and would have a cost. Cabling would be more reliable but would create disruption to the office while being installed, whereas a wireless network would be less disruptive to install but may be less reliable.

A cloud-based system such as KashCade will not require much in the way of installing the actual software, but it is important to verify that the broadband speed and existing computer capacity are compatible with the requirements of the system. There may be an additional requirement to upgrade hardware or to buy new terminals for the warehouse or sales staff. Currently, CCC only has four computers, so more will need to be purchased at a cost for the warehouse and sales staff and directors' access.

Transition costs

CCC would face some disruption while the new accounting system is installed and set up. CCC may need to pay for additional staff time to enter data for customers, suppliers and employees into the system so that it is fully operational, and it is anticipated that this could be completed within one week. This would potentially require an additional week of paid hours.

A further cost the company should consider, but one that is harder to quantify, is staff discontent at a change to the current system. Staff within the accounting team may be unhappy about needing to learn new working practices, increased controls and how to operate a new system. Other employees may see the increased controls in place as preventing them from carrying out their work, and unnecessary.

Procedure manuals cost

There would be a cost associated with producing procedure manuals to ensure staff know the expected working practices and procedures surrounding the new accounting system. There should also be a rota produced for cover when staff are absent. This should be completed by the senior accounts clerk as part of their normal role. As an estimate, this would take approximately 20 hours of their time per year.

Benefits

Increased information benefit

The first benefit to CCC would be the ability to produce reports from the centralised accounting system that provide complete information on the full financial position of the company. These reports can be reviewed on a regular basis by both the directors and the senior accounts clerk. The cash-related reports should help ensure cash flows are effectively managed. This will benefit the company by reducing overdraft fees and avoiding embarrassment with suppliers. The reports produced would include:

- Statement of profit or loss
- Statement of financial position
- Statement of cash flows
- Aged receivable analysis

- Cash flow forecast
- Supplier payment reports
- Costs by cost centre/code
- Analysis of petty cash expenditure
- Payroll reports
- Budgets and budgetary control reports

The financial statements could be prepared in draft format by the accounting team, reducing the input by the external accountancy firm, with a longer-term view to bringing the preparation of the financial statements in-house completely.

Cash flow benefits

An aged receivable analysis can be produced to strengthen the system of chasing overdue debts and ensure customers who have not paid are put on stop quickly. This will prevent customers from taking advantage of the current lax controls.

Cash flow forecasts will enable the directors and the senior accounts clerk to estimate the cash inflows to and outflows from the company, manage cash balances more effectively and reduce the overdraft and related fees. It will also assist with the planning of any significant cash expenditure. Overdraft fees and interest payments could be reduced each year.

Payroll security, accuracy and efficiency

The payroll will be accurately produced when required, with the benefit of the system being up-to-date payroll rules and regulations, such as tax rates. This will produce a benefit of more accuracy, fewer queries and increased efficiency of staff time, as well as compliance with RTI. It is estimated that the system will speed up the completion of the payroll each month. As HM Revenue & Customs (HMRC) requires monthly online payroll reporting, this will ensure that the process is made more efficient as Sonja does not need to type the monthly totals into the system (they will already be there and the software sends the information once it is ready and authorised for transmission).

Disaster recovery

There will be less danger from a system breakdown with appropriate backup of a central system. If one computer were to fail then the other staff could continue working, and a support agreement would ensure that, if the main system failed, it could be operational again as quickly as possible with less risk of lost or corrupted data. Holding the data in the 'cloud' as KashCade's system does will ensure that upgrades are completed by KashCade rather than a member of the team at CCC having to install the necessary information.

Supplier relations

Another benefit would be improved supplier relations, as suppliers should be paid the correct amounts and on time. This could also benefit the credit terms and conditions that suppliers grant CCC, further improving cash flow.

If the suppliers offer prompt payment (settlement) discounts, these could be monitored and utilised by CCC thus making additional cost savings.

Fraud

Further benefits are the significant reduction in the risk of fraud and the improvement of controls within the system together with improved cost control. Central reports will assist both the owners and the senior accounts clerk with analysing payments and wages, and identifying where costs are higher than expected. Due to current poor controls, it is not known if CCC has suffered from fraudulent activities so benefits are hard to evaluate.

Morale

Another benefit is the improved morale of staff. The accounting team would benefit from training, including formal accounting training as requested, and this would improve their efficiency and effectiveness as well as morale. Better-motivated staff should result in lower staff turnover and also improved commitment to the company.

The morale of the non-accounting staff will be improved by the timely completion of accurate wages.

Regulations

A final benefit is that CCC will be able to comply with regulations such as the Data Protection Regulations with good, secure storage of its data and information. Payroll reporting will be automated and can be completed on time, and VAT returns (if appropriate) can be automatically calculated and sent to HMRC.

Activity 7: Issues during transition

Accounting system introduction:

- Training staff, cost and fear of new system – especially by some members of the team (eg warehouse staff) who may have had limited exposure to computerised inventory systems in the past
- Data loss during migration to the new system, or moving data which is incorrect across to the new package

  It is important to ensure that data moved onto the new system is correct and accurate. Customer and supplier details should be checked and balances verified. This will take time but it must be completed correctly to avoid issues later on.

Monthly reporting requirements:

- Increased pressure on staff at month end may lead initially to resistance to complete the necessary tasks.
- Risk of inaccurate information provided if staff are not trained and motivated to provide quality reports. It is important to explain to staff why this is required, and how it will help the company going forward.
- It is important to establish exactly what the departments need to report on, and where the initial focus will be. It would be a good idea for CCC to focus initially on key areas of weakness, for example cash flow and payments to suppliers, rather than reporting on all variables.
- The current staff has a mixture of accounting experience, with Stefan being a part-qualified accountant. It is important for the directors to ensure that the team are trained and fully understand what information is required. It is likely that CCC will have to invest in staff training in order to make any changes.

Recruitment of a qualified senior accountant:

- There could be resistance to the introduction of a new member of management, especially within the accounting team. This may be perceived by existing staff as a criticism of their current performance, breeding resentment and poor co-operation with the new accountant.

Activity 8: CCC new accounting system

Ethical

- The AI-driven sales ledger may make decisions that are biased and compromise the ability of legitimate customers to secure credit with CCC. This may affect the company's reputation (especially if any existing customers have their credit facilities rescinded and the company is unable to justify it).
- A cloud-based system may have cybersecurity weaknesses which may affect the integrity and confidentiality of the data used by CCC. Any breaches may be damaging in both financial and reputational terms.

Sustainable

- The new system will reduce the amount of paper generated by the company when producing reports.
- The new hardware will include a server, meaning that there will be greater electricity costs associated with the new system.

Social

- The shift to working patterns (2pm–10pm) may not be compatible for the anticipated users of the new accounting system (plus there is a risk that information may not be available at times that CCC might require it).
- There is no project manager appointed which may compromise a successful transition to the new system and create difficulties for staff.

Corporate

- Although savings are being promised, they are only quoted as being 'up to' 20% of existing costs that 'could' be saved. This may not be substantiated and could even lead to additional costs being incurred.
- There is an expectation that the new system will be compatible with existing systems, but again this is not definitive (and, as above, the absence of a project manager may make the transition and testing process more stressful for staff than it should be).

Environmental

- Investing in new hardware means that existing hardware is likely to need to be scrapped and unless it can be re-purposed, it may need to go to landfill.

> **Tutorial note.** There will inevitably be cross-over between different categories (eg considering electricity costs as an environmental factor) plus other points that are not covered here may also be valid. Sensible answers should be rewarded as long as they clearly describe the implications of the change in relation to the stated categories.

Test your learning

1 Ard Ltd (Ard) is a large business with many operating centres. To date, its accounting has been done using various software packages on an independent PC at each operating centre. Ard now plans to move to a centralised accounting function with an integrated accounting system.

Required

Complete the following statement.

Ard's plan is [▼] change.

Picklist

- A systematic
- A transformational
- An incremental

2 **Complete the following statement.**

The fact that Ard's accounting staff in its operating centres will no longer use the skills they have developed in accounting is:

	✓
a tangible cost of the change.	
an intangible benefit of the change.	
a tangible benefit of the change.	
an intangible cost of the change.	

3 **Complete the following statement.**

The fact that Ard's employees will be disrupted by the planned change, so will not be able to work on an alternative new project and may even be distracted from their other tasks, is an

[▼] of the change.

Picklist

- Inevitable consequence
- Intangible benefit
- Opportunity cost

4 In the process of integrating its accounting system, Ard has discovered some misappropriation of assets and has dismissed the accountant responsible.

Required

Complete the following statement.

This is an example of [▼] change.

Ensuring the system is effective following such a change is likely to take [▼].

Picklist

- A forced
- An agreed
- Little time
- Some time

5 **Complete the following statement.**

Change should be [▼] in that the benefits of the change should outweigh its costs.

Picklist

- Cost effective
- Cost efficient
- Cost neutral

6 There are several situations which may cause an organisation to review their controls and accounting systems.

Required

Using the picklist provided, select the correct answer for each of the following situations

	Reason
A merger of the treasury and the finance function	▼
Management accounts report that the costs for the warehouse department are consistently running above budget	▼
The sales team to be issued with tablet devices to allow them to place orders and check inventory levels, whilst with customers in the showroom	▼
The directors are discontinuing one of the less profitable products, resulting in a refocus on the remaining three core products instead	▼

Picklist

- Company strategy change
- Financial change
- Personnel change
- Technological change

7 SWOT analysis is used to analyse the implications of changes made to the accounting system.

Required

Identify whether the following statements about SWOT analysis are true or false.

	True ✓	False ✓
The financial performance of a company should be considered as one of its strengths.		
The emergence of a new competitor has been identified as a weakness to a company in a recent board report.		
A company has recently invested in artificial intelligence (AI) technology to screen customers for poor credit risks. The directors consider this to be an opportunity to increase revenue.		

Test your learning answers

Chapter 1

1 A statement of cash flows shows receipt of a loan as part of [financing activities] and proceeds from the disposal of non-current assets as part of [investing activities].

2 The correct answers are:

	Ethical ✓	Environmental ✓
Improving recycling rates in the factory by 30% year on year		✓
Changing supplier who can supply the materials 20% cheaper, but with less control over the supply chain	✓	
Installing a carbon capture unit on the main factory costing £2 million		✓
Introducing a more generous pension scheme for employees	✓	

All of the decisions will impact the company on a financial or economic basis, either short term or long term (eg the pension scheme commitments and the carbon capture capital installation). It may be argued that treating staff more favourably by allowing them access to a better pension scheme would be an ethical decision made by the organisation. Equally, changing the supplier to one whose supply chain may be less transparent could help the profitability of an organisation, but may adversely affect its ethical stance (consider the real-life examples where high street fashion chains have sourced their clothing from less reputable companies, and faced a harsh public response as a result). Improving recycling rates and reducing carbon emissions will have an environmental impact as well as a financial one.

3 The correct answers are:

- According to Mendelow's Matrix, stakeholders with high levels of power and low levels of interest should be kept informed. - **False**
- Suppliers tend to want fair terms of trade with customers who display realistic prospects of success. - **True**
- One example of an internal stakeholder is a shareholder. - **True**
- Another example of an internal stakeholder is a lender. - **False**

According to Mendelow's Matrix, stakeholders with low levels of power and high levels of interest should be kept informed – those with high levels of power and low levels of interest (eg government or customers) should be kept **satisfied**.

Suppliers do want fair terms of trade with an organisation that has a future, or else it may be trading with a customer that cannot pay its debts.

Although they may not be like other internal stakeholders (eg managers or employees) who operate within the organisation, shareholders are still directly connected and are therefore internal stakeholders.

However, due to their relationship being more about the supply of capital (and as such, similar to any other supplier) lenders are **external** stakeholders.

4 The correct answer is:

	✓
Statement of financial position	
Statement of profit or loss	
Statement of changes in equity	✓
Statement of cash flows	

The statement of changes in equity is described as follows:

'A reconciliation of the opening and closing equity balances for the reporting period. It enables stakeholders to see the impact of new share issues, profit or loss for the period and dividends paid to equity shareholders.'

5

Description	Type of report
A company's main objective, and its purpose, strategy and values	Mission statement
The norms and standards of behaviour that express the organisation's identity and help it to achieve its objectives	Ethical reporting
A way of reporting financial, ethical and sustainability factors	Integrated reporting

Although some of these sound similar, there are some differences. Mission statements are usually brief and focused on key themes. Ethical reporting may include sustainability goals, but it is fundamentally about desirable forms of behaviour. Similarly, integrated reporting is a mixture of financial and non-financial reporting.

If you struggled with this question, please refer to the relevant section within the chapter.

6 The correct answers are:

- A report produced by consultants that describes the technology infrastructure changes by industry in the next ten years - **Strategic**
- The individual feedback from one customer experience - **Operational**
- Analysis of feedback from all customer experiences - **Tactical**
- The balance on the sales ledger - **Operational**

Long-term information (especially in relation to industry-wide changes in technology) is almost guaranteed to be strategic.

Customer feedback can produce varying forms of information: the feedback from one customer is likely to be a snapshot in time, and would most likely be operational in nature, while analysis of all customers is more likely to illustrate more tactical information.

Sales ledger information could be strategic (eg do your customers buy your products) but without the counter-balance of the information relating to products that remain unsold (and the reasons why) it is unlikely that this balance alone would be considered strategic information. Sales ledger balances can also provide information that is of a tactical nature (eg whether the credit control function is operating satisfactorily) but would need wider analysis to be meaningful. Consequently, a balance is likely to provide only limited information that is useful in the short-term, making it most likely to be operational in nature.

Chapter 2

1

Action	Type of control activity
Person A matches dispatch notes to invoices; Person B creates invoice to customer	Segregation of duties
Control account reconciliation	Arithmetic and accounting control
Petty cash box kept locked	Physical control
Adequate resourcing of accounting function	Organisational control
Review of budgetary control report	Management control

2 Management should regularly ensure that staff perform **reconciliations** of the receivables ledger to ensure accuracy and completeness of the data.

3 Allocating one customer's payment to another customer's account in order to balance the books and detract from a shortfall is called **teeming and lading** .

4

Situation	Fraud triangle condition
'They never check on the older items in the warehouse, so they're the easiest ones to steal.'	Opportunity
'I've worked so hard for this company over the years and yet no-one notices. I'm definitely entitled to take items out of the stationery cupboard for my own personal use.'	Rationalisation
'If I don't find the money in the next week, my house will be repossessed by the building society. I have to steal cash from the safe because I have no other way of finding the money I owe.'	Pressure

Dishonesty could be considered a way of rationalising fraudulent activity, but we are working from the Cressey fraud triangle and this term is not used.

5 The correct answers are:

	✓
Morale	✓
Social	
Reputation	✓
Environmental	
Financial	✓

6 The correct answers are:

	✓
Time	
Responsibility	
Likelihood	✓
Volatility	
Impact	✓

7 The correct answer is:

	✓
During the analysis of the sales system, a fraud matrix graded the potential loss from misappropriation to be rated 5. Management have decided urgent action is required.	✓
A fraud matrix is a subjective analysis of an organisation's controls, and will ensure that all recommendations identified are actioned immediately.	
A control within the payroll system has been rated as 2 within the fraud matrix. Management have decided that this risk must be rectified immediately.	

A fraud matrix enables the prioritisation of the key risks, focusing on the most significant first. An organisation will then deal with the highest risks first, which is why a fraud matrix grades the risks rather than dealing with all of the weaknesses at the same time.

A fraud matrix rates the lowest risk as 1 and the highest as 5, therefore anything rated 5 should be prioritised over lower rated risks.

Chapter 3

1 The correct answers are:

	✓
Cost effectiveness	✓
Ease of use	
Reliable	✓
Providing timely information	✓

Ease of use is not a specific objective of an accounting system – although, it is fair to say that this would be a desirable feature. The accounting system should meet the requirements of the organisation in providing reliable and timely information in a cost-effective manner.

2 The requirement for an accountant to act diligently is part of the fundamental principle of

professional competence and due care .

Professional competence and due care: Having the right level of current professional knowledge and skill to give competent professional service, and **acting diligently** and in accordance with applicable and professional standards.

3 Management should regularly ensure that staff perform [reconciliations] of the receivables ledger to ensure accuracy and completeness of the data.

4 Control objectives in relation to taking orders and extending credit are part of the [sales] system of the accounting system.

5 Completion of GRNs is a control activity related to the control objective of [only accepting goods and services that have been ordered and appropriately authorised].

The correct option is the only one that includes the core information of matching an authorised purchase order.

6 The correct answers are:

- The payroll clerk manually recalculates all their own work to confirm the accuracy of the payroll. - **Would not help**
- Wages are automatically calculated by the payroll system which takes the number of hours worked by each employee from their swipe-card data and applies an hourly rate that is part of the system's master files. - **Would help**
- The total amount payable for each month's payroll is reviewed and authorised for payment by the chief accountant. - **Would help**

While the payroll clerk is offering to confirm the accuracy of their own work, it displays a lack of segregation of duties and also introduces the risk of manual error – both of which would not be considered helpful in ensuring accuracy.

However, introducing both automated and manual processes for confirming the accuracy of the payroll would help ensure that payments were accurate.

Chapter 4

1 Ard's plan is [a transformational] change.

The scale of change makes this transformational and not incremental. Systematic change may be used anecdotally, but it is not a term that is used in this context.

2 The correct answer is:

	✓
a tangible cost of the change.	
an intangible benefit of the change.	
a tangible benefit of the change.	
an intangible cost of the change.	✓

This does not have a financial cost but does demonstrate the loss of certain skills which the company may need should the new system malfunction in some way or a decision is subsequently taken to reverse this decision.

3 The fact that Ard's employees will be disrupted by the planned change, so will not be able to work on an alternative new project and may even be distracted from their other tasks, is an [opportunity cost] of the change.

Opportunity cost is the value of an activity that has not taken place, because of a decision to do something else, so the absence of other work due to the change must be quantified.

4 This is an example of [a forced] change.

Ensuring the system is effective following such a change is likely to take [some time] .

The need to dismiss the perpetrator in this instance was not planned or agreed, and the fact that fraud has taken place means care should be taken to confirm there are no further instances that the company needs to identify.

5 Change should be [cost effective] in that the benefits of the change should outweigh its costs.

This is the logic behind cost-benefit analysis. Remember though, not all costs or benefits are tangible, making the evaluation of cost-effectiveness potentially complex.

6

	Reason
A merger of the treasury and the finance function	Personnel change
Management accounts report that the costs for the warehouse department are consistently running above budget	Financial change
The sales team to be issued with tablet devices to allow them to place orders and check inventory levels, whilst with customers in the showroom	Technological change
The directors are discontinuing one of the less profitable products, resulting in a refocus on the remaining three core products instead	Company strategy change

Hopefully, these are all self-explanatory.

Please refer to the relevant section at the start of the chapter to confirm your understanding.

7 The correct answers are:

	True ✓	False ✓
The financial performance of a company should be considered as one of its strengths.	✓	
The emergence of a new competitor has been identified as a weakness to a company in a recent board report.		✓
A company has recently invested in artificial intelligence (AI) technology to screen customers for poor credit risks. The directors consider this to be an opportunity to increase revenue.		✓

Financial performance is internal to the company so should be considered a strength.

Competitors are external to a company so would be considered as threats.

While there is an opportunity to reduce credit risk and therefore boost revenue, the investment has already occurred, meaning that the technology is internal and as such should be considered a strength.

Scenario

1 Cookridge & Cookridge Carpets Ltd

Company background and history

Cookridge & Cookridge Carpets Ltd (CCC) is a large carpet and flooring dealership based in Southampton, UK. It is the main dealer for 'Umteeko' specialist vinyl flooring in the area and has been trading for four years. It was set up by two brothers, Peter and John Cookridge.

Peter is a trained carpet fitter and has worked in the industry for the past 20 years. Before going into business with his brother, he was the senior manager in a national carpet chain. John was recently made redundant from his role as a mining engineer.

The business was established using John's £80,000 redundancy money and an inheritance the brothers received. Peter managed to raise a loan of £60,000 (using his house as collateral) in 20X2 to refinance the business as the company's bank overdraft was getting large and expensive to maintain.

The brothers purchased a large plot of land on which they developed a building to use as the carpet and flooring showroom. They started out selling and fitting carpets, and then expanded into specialist flooring. This expansion was organised by Peter, who had developed excellent working relationships with carpet and vinyl manufacturers from his time in the industry.

In February 20X1, CCC was asked by Umteeko to become its main dealership for Southampton. Umteeko is a quality product commanding a premium price and requires fitters to have specialist training to fit it.

CCC's mission statement

> Our mission is to provide an excellent level of service to all of our customers – and we endeavour to offer our customers a quality product at a competitive price.
>
> We aim to act ethically towards our suppliers, customers and staff, ensuring the best in service and supporting diverse needs and requirements.
>
> The environment is important to us and we aim to recycle wherever possible. We promise to remove all of the packaging from customers' premises and dispose of this in an environmentally friendly way.

Developments in the market

The popularity of Umteeko has grown and, therefore, the supplier insists on reviewing its dealers on a regular basis. All fitters must be fully trained, and qualified fitters are required to attend a refresher course every two years. Umteeko requires that only its specialist adhesives are used in the fitting process to ensure its product guarantees are valid.

Carpets are declining in popularity in the UK market with the rise of allergies, and the difficulties of keeping carpets clean in a busy family home. Wood and laminate flooring, as well as specialist vinyl floors like Umteeko and its main competitor, Kleandarn, are increasing their market share.

The increase in large warehouse-style retailers has reduced smaller retailers' margins on many of the popular brands of carpet and vinyl. CCC is finding it hard to match the prices of the larger retailers on some of the products it is selling.

CCC's strategic planning and control

Strategy mapping

Strategy maps are tools used by organisations to consider how value is created. They evaluate connections between strategic objectives in the form of causes and effects. CCC uses strategy mapping to evaluate its future prospects – eg when discussing the ongoing viability of the business with the bank.

Staff

CCC's key personnel are as follows:

Director	John Cookridge
Director	Peter Cookridge
Wages clerk	Sonja Douglas (part-time)
Senior accounts clerk	Margaret Peterson (part-time)
Accounts receivable clerk	Stefan Kalinowski (part time)
Showroom and marketing manager	Jim Andrews
Warehouse and operations manager	Joe Bloggins (joined October 20X2)
Sales staff	Isaac Jackson (sales manager) Ron Sellers Kim Lee
Delivery drivers	Sasha Bilton Lynn Smith
Carpet fitters	Jake Brew Pritpal Iqbal John Smedley David Lee Paul Collins (can also fit vinyl and wood floors)
Vinyl fitters	Sally Burroughs (Umteeko trained) Alan Rogers (Umteeko trained) Jack Brundell

Peter's main hobby is building and racing motorbikes. He is a popular and well-known figure on the local motor-racing scene.

John is married to Paula, who acted as company secretary for the first two years of the company's existence. She then left CCC to train as a solicitor.

The financial statements have been prepared by a local accountancy firm, Bright & Co; however, the directors are planning on bringing the preparation of these within CCC's accounting department. The company does not require an audit.

Extracts from the financial statements of CCC as at 31 December 20X2

Statement of profit or loss for CCC for the year ended 31 December 20X2

	20X2 £'000	20X1 £'000
Revenue	1,106	930
Cost of sales	(703)	(633)
Gross profit	403	297
Salaries	(312)	(257)
Rent and rates	(30)	(30)
Other costs	(54)	(28)
Profit/loss from operations	7	(18)
Finance costs	(5)	(6)
Profit/loss before tax	2	(24)
Tax	–	–
Profit/loss for the period	**2**	**(24)**

Statement of financial position for CCC as at 31 December 20X2

	20X2 £'000	20X1 £'000
Assets		
Non-current assets	78	83
Current assets		
Inventory	85	61
Trade receivables	134	83
Bank and cash on hand	2	4
Total assets	299	231
Equity and liabilities		
Share capital	1	1
Retained earnings	65	63
Total equity	66	64
Non-current liabilities		
Loan	60	–
Current liabilities		
Trade payables	131	86
Bank overdraft	37	78
Accruals and other payables	5	3
Total liabilities	299	231

Extracts from the management accounts for year ending 31 December 20X2

	20X2		20X1	
	Carpets	Vinyl	Carpets	Vinyl
	£'000	£'000	£'000	£'000
Revenue	379	727	425	505
Cost of sales (including materials and staff)	(287)	(416)	(282)	(351)
Gross margin	92	311	143	154
	All products (£'000)		All products (£'000)	
Rent and rates		30		30
Salaries: Administration and management		87		87
Salaries: Sales		105		60
Salaries: Directors		120		110
Motor expenses		19		10
Irrecoverable debts		22		8
Other costs		18		16
Total costs		401		321
Net profit/(loss)		2		(24)

Other operational information

The carpet showroom's opening hours are as follows:

- Open six days a week
- Operates from 09:00 until 21:00, Monday to Saturday

The accounting function works from 09:00 until 17:30, Monday to Friday.

The accounting function office is located on the first floor of the showroom. Access to the office is by a set of stairs at the rear of the building. Toilet facilities for staff and customers are also on the first floor, so the stairs are used by members of the public.

Once on this floor, access to the accounting function office is easy because the keypad lock is never used – the accounts staff prefer to keep the door propped open. The accounting function office is open plan with no private working areas.

Both the brothers are key holders for the business. They hold the only full sets of keys, as one of them is always on the premises at close of business to ensure the property is secure. There is an alarm code they set every evening when they lock up.

Finance team

The accounting staff use the three computers (using a business version of Microsoft) purchased when the company was set up. In addition, a further two computers were purchased last year which are used by the warehouse team. The warehouse manager used the installation discs from his home computer to put an older version of Microsoft on to save the company some money. The computers are not part of a network.

They use spreadsheets for the bookkeeping and payroll calculations (HMRC tax tables are used by Sonja to ensure the correct tax is calculated). Stefan uses a template in Word to produce and print out the sales invoices.

The sales team place orders manually which go to Stefan who raises invoices. Customers are booked in for fitting (if required) or delivery.

Stefan backs up his sales data onto a small, separate hard drive. He has set up similar ones for payroll and purchases but is unsure whether Margaret and Sonja regularly use them. The aged receivables report is compiled by Stefan who enters the invoices onto an Excel spreadsheet. Any unpaid invoices which are over 35 days late are sent to a debt collection agency.

The finance team prepare quarterly management accounts, and these are given to management by the 20th of the month following the quarter end. The management accounts include a basic summary of the revenue and costs for the period, a budget control report and any other information requested by the management team; sometimes it is the aged receivables ledger and sometimes it is a review of the payroll costs.

Margaret is responsible for the company cheque book and keeps it in a drawer at her desk.

Fitting team

The delivery dates are set up by the sales team and discussed with the operations manager.

The fitters are then given a set amount of time to fit the flooring based on the product they are fitting; however, not all of the fitters work to the same standard and some are quicker than others. Some of the Umteeko fitters complain that there is not enough time to follow the full procedures required of the product.

Glossary

Chapter 1: Reporting and stakeholders

Corporate social responsibility reports: Outline the objectives for ensuring the ethical, sustainable and moral aims and achievements of the organisation.

External stakeholders: A group of stakeholders that includes customers, suppliers, banks and public groups, including government.

Internal stakeholders: A category of stakeholders that includes employees, management, and owners (eg shareholders).

Mission statement: A statement of a company's main objective, and its purpose, strategy and values.

Operational information: Information that is used to ensure that specific tasks are planned and carried out properly within an organisation. Operational information would consider matters such as cash receipts and payments, bank reconciliations and goods received and despatch notes.

Scorecard: A performance management tool which addresses all relevant areas of performance, both financial and non-financial, in an objective and unbiased fashion.

Stakeholder: Individuals or groups that, potentially, have an interest in what an organisation does.

Statement of cash flows: An analysis of how and why the company's cash balance has changed during a reporting period. In addition to the statement of financial position and the statement of profit or loss, it is important for both management and current and potential investors to understand how cash is being utilised by the business.

Statement of changes in equity: A reconciliation of the opening and closing equity balances for the reporting period. It enables stakeholders to see the impact of new share issues, profit or loss for the period and dividends paid to equity shareholders.

Statement of financial position: A list of all of the assets, liabilities and equity of the business at a particular point in time (the end of the reporting period).

Statement of profit or loss: A summary of the activity of the company during the reporting period (usually a year) comprising income and expenditure.

Strategic information: Information that is used to plan the objectives of the company and assess whether the objectives are being met. Strategic information is longer term by nature and may include market intelligence and competitor analysis.

Tactical information: Information that is used to decide how the resources of the business should be deployed and to monitor how efficiently they are being used. Tactical information could include cash flow forecasts and working capital management.

Chapter 2: Internal control systems and fraud

Accounting controls: Controls which help to identify mistakes in the accounting records.

Authorisation and approval of transactions: Undertaken by supervisors and managers. This shows the person processing the transaction that it is valid – eg overtime should be approved by departmental heads.

Authorisation controls: These ensure that only authorised personnel can make changes, such as to standing data or to authorise a bank payment.

Confidentiality: Not disclosing confidential information except in appropriate circumstances, and not profiting from confidential information.

Control activities: Policies and procedures that help ensure that objectives are carried out.

Control environment: Formed by the attitudes, awareness and actions of management and those responsible for ensuring that the internal controls within the organisation meet its needs.

Ethical values: Assumptions and beliefs about what constitutes 'right' and 'wrong' behaviour.

Ethics: A set of generally accepted principles that guide behaviour.

Fraud controls: Internal controls specifically against fraud in the areas of staff controls, management controls, physical controls and IT controls.

Fraud matrix: A map of the potential frauds against an organisation, cross-referenced to the risks of each of these occurring, documenting the controls over these risks. Also known as a risk matrix.

Fraud: A deliberate or intentional act to gain some form of advantage, or to cause loss to another party, from the use of deception.

Fundamental principles of professional ethics: The principles that underpin how a professional accountant should behave.

Integrity: Being straightforward and honest in all professional and business relationships.

Internal controls: Policies and procedures that address the risk that the aims and objectives of the organisation will not be met.

Misappropriation of assets: Theft, teeming and lading, payment of false employees/suppliers.

Misstatement of the financial statements: The overstatement of assets or profit, or the understatement of profit, losses or liabilities.

Monitoring, review and report: In this context, **monitoring** means looking at activity or behaviour related to a specified fraud risk because you need to know the extent of this activity or behaviour.

Review means gathering evidence of this activity or behaviour to understand the extent of this fraud risk.

Report means what you communicate to those higher up in the organisation as part of the overall risk management process.

Objectivity: Not allowing bias, conflict of interest or undue influence of others to override professional or business relationships.

Physical controls: Ensuring assets (eg inventory and cash) are safe via the use of locked doors, security cameras and inspections.

Professional behaviour: Complying with relevant laws and regulations and not bringing disrepute on the accounting profession (AAT, 2024).

Professional competence and due care: Having the right level of current professional knowledge and skill to give competent professional service, and acting diligently and in accordance with applicable and professional standards.

Reconciliations: Controls that check whether two different sources of information agree or that any differences are understood – eg bank reconciliations verifying the bank statement to the bank account on the nominal ledger.

Reviews: Performed by supervisors or managers by looking at summaries and reports of transactions – eg to ensure they are reasonable.

Risk assessment process: This includes the following: identify the risk; evaluate the risk; respond to the risk (manage/mitigate risk by taking appropriate action); ensure compliance (legal and regulatory); monitor, review and report.

Risk of fraud: The likelihood of the fraud occurring and its impact if it does occur.

Segregation of duties: Making sure that a number of people are involved in different parts of each process to minimise the opportunity for fraud and error.

System of internal control: The control environment, the entity's risk assessment process, the entity's processes to monitor the system of internal control, the information system and communication and control activities.

Systemic weaknesses: Weaknesses that arise within the accounting system itself, which leave it open to fraud and error.

Chapter 3: Accounting systems

Accounting system: A system that takes raw data on transactions as its input, processes this data, and then produces many outputs to meet the information needs of stakeholders.

Authorisation of transactions: This is a key control activity, indicating to accounting staff that the transaction in question is valid.

Cost effectiveness: This ensures that something is good value.

Information processing controls: Controls relating to the transactions and standing data in the computerised accounting system.

Integrity controls: To verify and validate input data, the processing of data and the production of reports.

Integrity of data: Ensures that data is complete, secure and accurate.

Physical controls: Ensure assets such as inventory and cash are safe.

Processing controls: May be used to warn the user if they try to log out before processing is finished or close a document prior to saving. Data is also checked for arithmetical accuracy.

Reliability: This ensures a process or system performs consistently well.

Risk: The threat to the company presented by the control objective not being attained.

Security controls: Controls in the accounting system that cover integrity controls, system controls and physical access controls.

Sustainability objectives: Goals or targets linked to desirable sustainability outcomes, activities and behaviour.

Sustainability practices: Policies, procedures and actions designed to support the achievement of an organisation's sustainability objectives.

System flowchart: A diagram that shows the flow of the accounting system using boxes and text to show the logic.

Timeliness: This means that the system should provide information at the required time.

User manual: An accurate analysis of how the accounting system and its controls operate, and how they should be used.

Chapter 4: Making changes

Cost-benefit analysis: Analyses recommendations for change in terms of the costs and benefits to the company of implementing them.

Incremental change: A small change or a big change made in small steps eg gradually moving each sub-system onto an integrated accounting package.

Intangible benefits: Benefits of the change that are more difficult to identify and quantify, eg improved reputation for efficiency, improving the customer experience in a showroom, facilitating an increase in the amount of time spent browsing, or making conditions for staff better so that they are more motivated at work.

Intangible costs: Cannot be quantified in financial terms, where the costs of the change are more difficult to identify and quantify – eg the cost of lost custom as customers go elsewhere during the disruption caused by the change.

Risk assessment process: An evaluation of the risks to the achievement of the organisation's objectives.

SWOT analysis: A way for management to highlight the key issues, and review where the organisation has strengths and weaknesses and to consider any opportunities or threats, from internal and external sources.

Tangible benefits: May be more difficult to quantify than tangible costs, but easy to identify (eg less time spent creating invoices, improved efficiency).

Tangible costs: Identified, quantifiable costs of the change eg buying a new software package.

Transformational change: A wholesale change – eg integrating all accounting functions at a centralised location with a new computer system.

Bibliography

AAT (2019) Could you spot these 5 signs of financial crime? [Online] Available from: https://www.aatcomment.org.uk/aatpowerup/ethics-info/could-you-spot-these-5-signs-of-financial-crime/ [Accessed 23 February 2026]

AAT (2024) Code of Professional Ethics. [Online]. Available from: https://www.aat.org.uk/prod/s3fs-public/assets/AAT-Code-Professional-Ethics.pdf [Accessed 23 February 2026]

Companies Act 2006 (2006) [Online] Available from: https://www.legislation.gov.uk/ukpga/2006/46/contents [Accessed 23 February 2026]

Cressey, D. R. (1973) *Other People's Money*. Montclair, NJ: Patterson Smith

FCA (2019) NatWest fined £264.8 million for anti-money laundering failures. [Online] Available from: https://www.fca.org.uk/news/press-releases/natwest-fined-264.8million-anti-money-laundering-failures [Accessed 23 February 2026]

Fraud Act 2006 (2006) [Online] Available from: https://www.legislation.gov.uk/ukpga/2006/35/contents [Accessed 26 February 2026]

Jaguar Land Rover (2026) Website and Reimagine strategy. [Online] Available from: https://www.jlr.com/ [Accessed 26 February 2026]

IFRS Foundation (2026) IFRS [Online] Available from: https://www.ifrs.com [Accessed 26 February 2026]

John Lewis Partnership (2021) Annual Report and Accounts 2025. [Online] Available from: https://www.johnlewispartnership.co.uk/~/media/Files/J/john-lewis/corp/documents/jlp-plc-ara-2024-25.pdf [Accessed 23 February 2026]

Law Society, The (2020) Money Laundering Regulations 2017. [Online] Available from: https://www.lawsociety.org.uk/topics/anti-money-laundering/quick-guide-to-the-mlrs [Accessed 23 February 2026]

PR Newswire (2023) Optimove surveys: 70% of consumers prefer eco-friendly brands as 64% of brands say they have an environmental responsibility program. [Online] Available from: https://www.prnewswire.com/news-releases/optimove-surveys-70-of-consumers-prefer-eco-friendly-brands-as-64-of-brands-say-they-have-an-environmental-responsibility-program-301851861.html [Accessed 23 February 2026]

Reuters (2017) Tesco to pay £214m to settle false accounting charges. [Online] Available from: https://www.reuters.com/article/uk-britain-tesco-fraud-idUKKBN16Z0KD [Accessed 23 February 2026]

Rolls Royce (2025) Rolls-Royce completes agreements with investigating authorities. [Online] Available from: https://www.rolls-royce.com/media/press-releases/2017/17-01-2017-statement.aspx [Accessed 23 February 2026]

Index

Tell us what you think

Got comments or feedback on this book? Let us know.
Use your QR code reader:

Or, visit:
https://www.smartsurvey.co.uk/s/W30E6Y/

Need to get in touch with customer service?

www.bpp.com/request-support

Spotted an error?

https://learningmedia.bpp.com/pages/errata